Hin: The Quiet Beauty of Japanese Bamboo Art

Robert T. Coffland

Donald Doe

Photographs by Daniel Strong

Art Media Resources
Faulconer Gallery,
Grinnell College
TAI Gallery

Published on the occasion of the exhibition
Hin: The Quiet Beauty of Japanese Bamboo Art
Organized by the Faulconer Gallery, Grinnell College
January 27 to March 19, 2006

Curated by Robert T. Coffland and Donald Doe

Note: Japanese names are given in traditional order, surname first.
    For example, "Nakatomi" is the family name in Nakatomi Hajime.

Editor: Dottie Indyke
Photographer: Daniel Strong
Design, production and printing: CA Design, Hong Kong

© 2006 Textile Arts Inc., Faulconer Gallery, Grinnell College, and Art Media Resources

Published by Art Media Resources
1507 South Michigan, Chicago, IL 60605
info@artmediaresources.com
www.artmediaresources.com

in association with
Faulconer Gallery, Grinnell College
Bucksbaum Center for the Arts, 1108 Park Street, Grinnell, Iowa 50112
www.grinnell.edu/faulconergallery
and
TAI Gallery/ Textile Arts, Inc
1571 Canyon Rd., Santa Fe, NM 87501
www.textilearts.com

© 2006 Robert T. Coffland for "Japanese Bamboo Art and the West"
© 2006 Donald Doe for "Lines in Space: Japanese Baskets as Art"

All images in this catalogue of work by Honda Syoryu, Kawashima Shigeo,
Kosuge Hounsai Kogetsu, and Tanioka Shigeo are copyright © Lloyd E. Cotsen.

ISBN: 58886-090-6 Hardcover
ISBN: 58886-091-4 Softcover

Front Cover: Fujinuma Noboru, *Adorned Heart* (detail), 2004. Collection of the late Myron Szold and Pam Crutchfield.

Back Cover: Shono Tokuzo, *Waves of Swaying Rice Plants* (detail), 2001. Collection of Eric and Karen Ende.

Pages 6, 14, 15: Honda Syoryu, *Dance* (details), 2000. Reproduced from the collection of,
and with permission of Lloyd E. Cotsen.

Pages 7, 9, 90: Ueno Masao, *Rotation of Ellipse Makes Two Transparent Drums* (details), 2004.
The Ruth & Sherman Lee Institute for Japanese Art at the Clark Center.

Pages 11, 13: Abe Motoshi, *Ocean Current* (details), 2000. Collection of Eugenie and Lael Johnson.

TABLE OF CONTENTS

Dedicated to Lloyd E. Cotsen and all of the collectors and museums in the
West whose support for the Japanese bamboo artists helps to
keep alive this precious and unique part of Japan's culture.

In memory of Myron R. Szold, 1935–2005. His delight in Japanese bamboo art was always a joy to behold.

ACKNOWLEDGEMENTS

LESLEY WRIGHT, DIRECTOR
FAULCONER GALLERY, GRINNELL COLLEGE

Hin: The Quiet Beauty of Japanese Bamboo Art was on view at the Faulconer Gallery, Grinnell College (Iowa) from January 27 through March 19, 2006, but the exhibition will live on in this lovely book. To bring the exhibition and catalogue to fruition, I have many people to thank.

The idea for the exhibition was originally proposed by Donald Doe, Lecturer in Art at Grinnell College in 2004 after a visit to TAI Gallery in Santa Fe. Subsequent conversations with Robert T. Coffland, director of TAI Gallery, brought about the collaboration which resulted in this exhibition. Dr. Doe's vision and Mr. Coffland's years of experience with Japanese bamboo art brought the exhibition into being and we are extraordinarily grateful to them.

Hin: The Quiet Beauty of Japanese Bamboo Art celebrates the work of 37 Japanese artists, all of whom we salute for their creativity and skill. The exhibition also celebrates the passion of American collectors of this art form. Their interest in Japanese bamboo art greatly expands the market for these incredible artists and allows them to push their art to new heights and in new directions. We would like to thank our lenders from across the country:

Arthur and Diane Abbey, New York
John and Mary Louise Bailey, Virginia
Barbara Billings and Ernest Vogel, Washington
Buchbinder Family Collection, Illinois

Carolyn Swartz and Matthew Bucksbaum, Illinois
Betsy and Edward Cohen, Pennsylvania
Lloyd and Margit Cotsen and the Cotsen Collection, California
The late Myron Szold and Pamela Crutchfield, Illinois
Eric and Karen Ende, California
Walter and Celia Gilbert, Massachusetts
Bradley Gordon, in memory of Angelique Leibow, California
Robert O. and Ritalou Harris, Maryland
Lael & Eugenie Johnson, Illinois
William J. & Marjorie R. Salman, New Mexico
Loretta Thurm, Illinois

Two institutions also loaned works from their collections: The Ruth & Sherman Lee Institute for Japanese Art at the Clark Center (Hanford, California), and the Museum of Arts and Design (New York, New York). We are delighted to collaborate with both of them on this project. Including bamboo art in their public collections further demonstrates its importance as an art form to be treasured.

The staff at TAI Gallery and the staff at the Faulconer Gallery are to be commended for attending to the myriad details that go into realizing an exhibition. In particular, Steve Halvorsen, Susi Perry and Okada Koichiro at TAI Gallery made our lives immensely easier with all their expertise. Milton Severe designed the exhibition at Grinnell College and Karla Niehus planned a rich array of programming. Special kudos go to Daniel Strong, Associate Director and Curator of Exhibitions, for tackling the exacting task of photographing all the pieces for the catalogue. We also salute the administration, faculty and students, particularly in the Chinese and Japanese Department, at Grinnell College for all their support.

Finally we thank Rosanne Chan of CA Design in Hong Kong for realizing our vision for this book, and Jeffrey Moy of Paragon Books for making sure it would have a wider distribution and long life.

LINES IN SPACE: JAPANESE BASKETS AS ART

BY DONALD DOE

Japanese basket makers (*kagoshi*) have been skillfully plaiting bamboo for millennia. A number of baskets, sealed with lacquer and dating between 2000 and 1000 BCE have been found in late Paleolithic sites. Those, of course, served practical purposes. By the eighth century CE those purposes included holding flower petals used in religious ceremonies; by the ninth, with the introduction of tea from China, baskets were used for tea storage, sweets, and flowers associated with the tea ceremony.[1]

Chinese culture was greatly admired in Japan—and would be for centuries. Imported Chinese paintings, ceramics and baskets, collectively called *karamono* and understood to reflect the tastes of the highly cultured Chinese literati, were prized. It is thus hardly surprising that *karamono* baskets, specifically to hold flowers in connection with the tea ceremony, were diligently copied by the most skilled of Japanese *kagoshi*.

In the Edo period (1615-1868, CE), Japanese society changed greatly; the merchant class, once ranked below peasants, became powerfully wealthy. As was true in Europe, this class sought to emulate the aristocracy. The popularity of the tea ceremony spread widely and, especially with the maturation of *Ikebana,* the art of flower arranging, the demand for baskets of very high quality increased greatly. In the ensuing Meiji period (1868-1912) as a modernizing Japan emerged, that demand continued to

spread through an ever-wider segment of the population.

Through much of this time, basket making changed little. There was, of course, a very great difference between baskets woven by some farmers during the winter months, and those intended for flower arrangements or for the *Chanoyu,* and later, the *Sencha* tea ceremonies. In any case, bamboo basket making was understood to be a utilitarian craft, at least to an important degree. Many baskets, of course, served the ordinary service of toting and storing all sorts of things, though it is true that rustic baskets were often highly regarded. But even the most exquisite were viewed as primarily functioning in service to other arts, which meant that bamboo art was considered secondary.

Whatever the status, Moroyama Masanori, chief curator of the National Museum of Modern Art in Tokyo, asserts that Japanese *kagoshi* closely imitated treasured Chinese models until well into the 20th century.[2] That commitment to tradition meant that Japan fostered masters of extraordinary virtuosity. Indeed, to this day, the Japan Craft Arts Association (the association that names National Living Treasures of Bamboo Art) honors mastery of traditional styles and traditional techniques.

At the same time, beginning in the latter part of the 19th century, Japanese masters especially in the Kansai region, which embraces both Osaka and Kyoto,

were becoming emancipated, so to speak, from the dominance of Chinese influence. This process of transformation gathered speed in postwar Japan. All of the arts, most notably painting and ceramics, were profoundly influenced by the arts of the West—perhaps most conspicuously by the emergence of Abstract Expressionism. Works in bamboo changed somewhat more gradually than other media, not because its traditions were more binding, but because there was nothing at all like Japanese bamboo basketry in the art practices of postwar United States, or, indeed, anywhere else. But adding structure and impetus to the process of change was the revival of the Nitten, originally formed in 1919 as the Imperial Art Exhibition. Reformed in 1958 and again the next year, the Nitten placed as much emphasis on originality and innovation as the Japan Craft Art Association placed on command of traditional techniques. It generated an exhibit which was divided into categories for the various arts—including Western Style Painting, Western Style Ceramics, and Craft Arts, which included bamboo baskets. Moroyama points to only a few bamboo artists of that moment who broke decisively with tradition (though it is ever thus; for example, only two artists, George Braque and Pablo Picasso, wrought the Cubist revolution in the visual arts). Among those few was Shono Shounsai (1904-1974), for a time a member of the Nitten world, but who returned to the

Japan Craft Art Association and was named the first Living National Treasure in bamboo arts.

His legacy is one that stamps this exhibition. Shono Tokuzo is his son, Fujinuma Noboru, Tanioka Shigeo, and Nakatomi Hajime, all included in *Hin*, were among the many inspired by the elder Shono to become artists working in bamboo. Both Abe Kiraku Motoshi and Yamaguchi Ryuun were his students.

Given the ancient character of this tradition in "craft art" and the astounding vitality that it now contains, it seems hard to believe there are today perhaps fewer than 200 artisans and artists working in bamboo in all of Japan. Perhaps one reason lies in the fact that mastering the art of transforming poles of bamboo into exquisite objects is a dauntingly complex and demanding process. Usually and inevitably, the artist's training takes years. Usually, too, it takes many more before the artist wins the recognition provided by important prizes at exhibitions. A glimpse of a few careers underscores the general point.[3]

Maeda Chikubosai II, named a Living National Treasure in 1995 when he was close to 80 years old, was taught not by his famed father but by his father's students. His father then sent him away, to Hawaii and Korea, to represent his family business, before offering recognition to him. He won admission to important exhibitions after the war, but it was not until 1972 that he was granted full membership in the Japan Craft Arts Association.

Hayakawa Shokosai V, born in Osaka in 1932, began training with his father in 1951. He trained half a decade in preparing bamboo before he was allowed to make his first basket—and did not win his first solo exhibition until 1965. Higashi Takesonosai began his apprenticeship in 1931, at the age of 16. Almost two decades passed before he was admitted to the Nitten of 1969— at the age of 35—and won the grand prize. Still, he was not admitted to full membership of the Japan Traditional Craft Arts Association until 1994, when he was nearly 80. Kajiwara Koho began his apprenticeship at the age of 17. That apprenticeship lasted ten years, as it did for Tanioka Shigeo who, at the age of 25, apprenticed himself to Tanabe Chiuunsai II.

And so it went, for nearly all of the 37 artists in this exhibition. Further, Kajiwara Aya, who is the first woman working in bamboo to become a full member of the Japan Craft Arts Association, asserts, "Many bamboo artists must take part-time jobs... . I myself have a part-time job helping at a rest home. You cannot become rich as a bamboo artist, even if your work wins awards of excellence."[4]

Yet further, mastery in bamboo itself is measured against splendid works often treasured for centuries as well as contemporary pieces by artists who have been working for decades. Standards are very, very high. (Given the cultural values involved, perhaps it is small wonder that by far the most reliable automobiles on the planet come from the island nation of Japan.)

There is perhaps another reason for the small number of great bamboo artists, and that too is cultural: even today, though there are two Living National Treasures of Bamboo Art and major exhibitions are held in Japan, baskets still exist in a kind of cultural alcove. In 1966, a major Japanese publishing firm, in conjunction with the Agency for Cultural Affairs, began publishing the Japanese Arts Library. It was meant for Western readers. It drew upon the collections of the three great national museums—in Kyoto, Nara, and Tokyo. It was supplied with scholarship of the first rank and at its inception was meant to include 30 volumes. They ranged from folk art, to Bugaku masks, to Shinto architecture, to Japanese swords, tea bowls and textile dyeing. But no volume was planned for the extraordinary tradition of bamboo art. Making this yet more curious is the fact that bamboo may be the most prevalent cultural image in Japan, appearing in scroll paintings, tea bowls, textiles, stationary and so on. The list is nearly endless.

Given the variety of culturally prized objects classified as art, it may seem more or less inexplicable that the bamboo arts were—and continue to be—categorized as "craft." To be sure, the tradition of Japanese baskets of elegant facture is rooted in baskets meant to hold flowers and many of the works in this show, though not all, can fulfill that function. To be equally sure, the normative division between art and craft, in both the East and West, rests on precisely that ground of functionality. For an object to be classified as art, its reason for being must be aesthetic (in some sense of the word) rather than pragmatic.

But for at least half a century it has been clearly understood that an aesthetic response to a given work rests not on some essential quality within it, but with the context in which it is presented. Away from a gallery or museum setting, with no attendant lighting or labels, and in the absence of any awareness of an artist's identity, many contemporary works might appear to be an oddly interesting collection of debris, a group of unsorted vacation photos or a stack of consumer products. In sum, there would be no particular reason to identify them as works of art at all.

It is here that the classification of Japanese bamboo baskets as craft begins to collapse. In every sense, that is, these works are encountered as art. In the Faulconer Gallery and in the homes of the collectors, these works are shown and prized as aesthetic objects.[5] The extraordinary command of technique, which these works clearly evince, is not a display of technical mastery for its own sake. Rather, technique is employed to create the forms and plays of texture that the artist has imagined. That mastery is almost surely a source of pleasure and wonder for any careful viewer, but that response radiates to the whole that it creates and, probably simultaneously, to no small amount of appreciation for the cultural values that support and perpetuate it. Small wonder that contemporary Japanese bamboo artists have rejected the term *kagoshi* for *takekogeika* or *chikugeika*, both terms meaning, literally, bamboo craft artists.

The Western viewer will probably be unable to resist seeing a number of these works purely as sculpture. Nagakura Kenichi's *Bamboo Vastness* (p. 74-75) nearly denies craft, seeming to be an almost random, densely expressive weaving. Rubbed with gray-green clay that appears to be a patina on the lustrous bronze-colored bamboo, the whole suggests some ancient artifact shaped by the stresses of time and the weight of earth in which it was long buried. Mimura Chikuho's *Cloud on the Peak* (p. 86-87) relates to *Bamboo Vastness*, but is much more compact. The densely woven bamboo shape seems muscular, and at the same time a gleaming, abstracted cloud that offers a sense of the work expanding from its center, as though billowing outward.

The simple open weave of bamboo of *Kirin* (p. 76-77), created by Morigami Jin, offers a sharp contrast. Very delicate bamboo strands are made to curve and bend (one wants to say molded or folded) in complex ways that will remind many viewers of the reclining abstract figures of Henry Moore. At the same time, *Kirin* has about it a nearly casual air, a sculpture shaped by chance, as though loosely crumpled like paper and simply dropped.

Torii Ippo has woven two interlaced ribbons of bamboo for *Development— Piercing* (p. 30-31), one forming a loop in gleaming burgundy, the "ribbon" laced with dramatic wide bands of bamboo and pierced by another looping ribbon, this in the golden natural tone of the grass. Organic and supplied with a sense of eminent rising, yet at the same time complexly architectural, it possesses an uncanny sense of scale; one could see it as

an elegant maquette for an immense work of sculpture. Yamaguchi Ryuun's *Crashing Wave* (p. 46-47) is also a kind of three-dimensional ribbon, wide and long strands of bamboo, looking utterly fragile, curve into space, coiling around one another and suggesting one wave engulfing the next in a ceaseless flow. Equally suggestive of nature and natural forces, Kawashima Shigeo's *Cosmic Ring* (p. 80-81), (another extraordinarily delicate work) finds fine strands of bamboo tied together with black cotton thread. The small work seems to float, or at least be able to float in space, the leached bamboo glowing like a distant celestial object brought close by telescope.

Equally delicate, Honda Syoryu (p. 70-71) has wrought the path of compressed disks, twisting in space, creating a compelling visual puzzle kindred to the perspectival logic of a print by M.C. Escher. Like Honda's *Dance*, Ueno Masao's *Rotation of Ellipse Makes Two Transparent Drums* (p. 64-65) is an organic abstract sculpture that seems, in fact, to be nearly transparent and while seeming simple is visually very complex. At first glance, it looks as though the artist has created a monochromatic work burnished with a chestnut brown dye. In fact, the inner facet of the bamboo strands—cut thin as wire—are covered in gold leaf and given coat after coat of lacquer. As the viewer moves around the work, the gleam of light on gold and the rather widely spaced lines of the transparent drums seem to dance in a way that recalls Sol Lewitt's logical exercises with cubic outlines in white and their capacity to fracture into visual enigmas.

None of this is to imply that these works are the most important in the exhibition or to argue that Japanese bamboo art is to be understood as art on the grounds that it shares formal connections with western sculpture. Rather, the point is to underscore the varied and dynamic ways in which tradition has been extended to create dramatic, sculptural forms.

Works that are clearly baskets share this sculptural quality; the technical prowess of the maker transforms and greatly expands the very idea (as simple as it would seem to be) of basket. Fujinuma Noboru's *Adorned Heart* (p. 58-59) is really two baskets in one. For the interior basket, the four-part plaiting of the base almost magically becomes the weave of two strands of bamboo, and then one, creating a delicate, nearly transparent inner shape. The rhythmic interlaced pattern of the exterior seems to be made of much thicker ribbons of bamboo—but the graceful path of the interwoven strands is possible because each strand is, in fact, made up of a stack of six very slender strands of bamboo. Shono Tokuzo also stacks, but then meticulously fans leached bamboo in his *Waves of Swaying Rice Plants* (p. 54-55) to create a powerfully sculptural work. Nakatomi Hajime's *Fragrant Wind* (p. 88-89) is aptly named: it is as ethereal as dusk. Kajiwara Aya's basket is simply and directly titled *Spiral Pattern Flower Basket* (p. 48-49). It might seem simply and directly made, but that is an illusion. The band of golden weft strands that create the spiral swells to its greatest width at the basket's widest point, then diminishes gradually to close as a circle surrounding the opening and this woven spiral creates a second one, made of only the exposed dark warp strands of bamboo.

Katsushiro Soho, the bamboo artist most recently honored with the title Living National Treasure, is the maker of a boldly wrought basket titled *Playful* (p. 38-39). Like Fujinuma's work, this piece honors the tradition of rustic baskets and perhaps for excellent reason. He is both a basket maker and a farmer. A few years ago, he said, "I have a keen sense of the seasons. Observing nature, I obtain new themes for my baskets. The themes I choose are usually bright and joyful. The beauty of bamboo, to me, is the way it reveals a dynamic line in space. I honor traditional techniques, but I think the development of new techniques is also very important."[6]

Looking carefully (probably most gallery visitors and readers of this volume will feel the urge to find his or her favorite work), Katsushiro's views seem to apply quite aptly to every work, whether primarily an abstract sculpture in bamboo or quite clearly a flower basket. A sense of nature is pervasive in these works of woven grasses. In their luster and technical elegance there is a celebration of both centuries-old tradition and the quite new transformation of it. Standing back, one can see the bamboo, curved, woven, flowing or enclosing, as lines in space. And many of these skillfully wrought lines do describe baskets, now primarily meant as art objects in their own right, containing a quiet beauty as remarkably as, traditionally, they held flowers.

1   Toshiko McCallum, exhibition catalogue, *Containing Beauty: Japanese Bamboo Flower Baskets*, (Los Angeles: UCLA Museum of Cultural History, 1988) 14-15. Much of the history of Japanese basketry is drawn from that admirably scholarly publication.

2   *Kateigaho*, International Edition, Sekai Bunka Publishing, Inc. (Autumn, 2005) 102.

3   Robert T. Coffland, *Contemporary Japanese Bamboo Arts* (Chicago: Art Media Resources and Santa Fe: TAI Gallery, 1999). The interested reader may find expanded biographies of 19 of the artists included in this exhibition in Coffland's book.

4   Coffland, p. 60.

5   For an extended and highly knowledgeable appreciation of the aesthetic pleasures of these works, see Lloyd Cotsen's essay, "Japanese Bamboo Baskets: The Visual and the Visceral," in the sumptuous *Japanese Bamboo Baskets: Masterworks of Form and Texture* (Los Angeles: Cotsen Occasional Press, 1999) 10-29.

6   Coffland, p. 66.

Japanese Bamboo Art And The West

by Robert T. Coffland

What is it about this art form that has ignited so much interest among Western viewers and collectors? For many, it is the simple attraction of the vessel form. For thousands of years human beings have employed and created vessels for daily life. Our ability to craft containers is a critical step in our evolution, so we are drawn to them on a primal level. We derive special pleasure from vessel forms that have no function other than portraying beauty.

Certainly we are fascinated by the transformation of a mundane material like bamboo into a dazzling and complex array of sophisticated shapes and forms— bamboo that resembles wood, leather, metal, and grass, for instance. Each vessel is as mysterious and intriguing as a woven textile or a piece of music. I have often heard collectors and artists speak of their amazement at the limitless possibilities of a stick of bamboo. Since I became interested in this art form, I have not made a single trip to Japan without seeing something surprisingly different made from bamboo. Viewers immediately grasp the staggering effort and depth of commitment necessary for artists to develop the skills to make even a simple basket. The time involved to reach the level of mastery is measured in decades, not years. In our age of mass-produced consumer goods, Japanese bamboo art harkens back to an earlier time when objects were imbued with the quality of human fingers interacting with natural material.

Underlying all of the above is the fact that no other culture in human history has so elevated the making of fiber vessel and sculptural forms. This formidable artistic creativity began in the late 19th century and continues to grow and blossom to this day. Westerners are drawn to Japanese bamboo art because of its aesthetic. The flexibility of bamboo allows compositions of volume and space that move the underlying basket into the sculptural realm. Use of varied widths of bamboo strips, innovative construction techniques, dyes, and original design concepts combine to forge an experience that one collector likened to walking in a Japanese garden, where something new is revealed at every turn. Others speak of the quiet beauty of well-proportioned forms. One individual, who collects all types of art, remarked that bamboo sculpture is an antidote to the harshness and coldness of contemporary art, where the skills of the artist are often considered virtually irrelevant.

The burgeoning interest of Westerners has reached a point where many artists find a far more receptive audience for their work outside Japan. This has, in turn, inspired more creative exploration of bamboo as an art-making material and bodes well for the next generation of Japanese bamboo artists.

Western interest in Japanese bamboo art can be traced to the 19th century and the Meiji restoration that brought Japan back into contact with the outside world. The new government slowly began encouraging industry and foreign trade. Commencing in 1862, Japanese arts and crafts were displayed at world fairs, which led to a great demand for all types of Japanese goods, including bamboo baskets. To promote trade, the Meiji administration sponsored Domestic Industry Exhibitions where awards were given to recognize excellence in various crafts. Basket dealers in Yokohama formed export businesses that sold to foreign visitors, which in turn led to the production of standardized baskets.

In the last quarter of the 19th century, artists such as Hayakawa Shokosai I, Wada Waichisai I, Tanabe Chikuunsai I, and Iizuka Hosai I gained recognition for their original bamboo artworks. They primarily crafted flower baskets and offering trays for the upper classes but also exhibited their work at the Domestic Industry Exposition in Tokyo. These government-sponsored exhibitions, which were juried by experts and peers, played an integral part in motivating artists to create new work. The prestige of winning prizes helped establish their pricing structures and legitimized their careers. These exhibitions have become even more vital in post-war Japan, as Japanese interest in bamboo has precipitously declined.

The first serious collector of bamboo was Swiss businessman Hans Sporry who, in the late 1800s, amassed over 2,000 bamboo related objects, including baskets, with a passion that would define the remainder of his life. Sporry's acquisition fervor soon carried him to Kyoto, Tokyo,

and other Japanese cities. One of the more intriguing aspects of his collection is that there are no pieces by Hayakawa, Wada, Tanabe, or Iizuka. Was Sporry not aware of the Domestic Industry Exhibitions or did he purposely choose not collect these artists? Perhaps it was a matter of funds, since the top bamboo artists' baskets commanded prices comparable to the artwork of the best potters and ceramicists. In 1903, after he returned to Switzerland, Sporry published a book about his collection and later wrote several additional books, including an autobiography. His collection now resides in the University of Zurich's Ethnographic Museum.

Another important collection was assembled by a 19th-century British businessman who bought bamboo baskets from Arima, a spa town outside of Osaka. His pieces are now housed at the Victoria and Albert Museum in London. During the Chicago World's Fair of 1893 the Japanese pavilion featured demonstrations and sales by bamboo artisans but, sadly, none of these pieces wound up at the Field Museum (later, the museum was given a

collection of bamboo baskets that was assembled in Japan during the 1940s and '50s). There is a smattering of small collections in European and American museums—including one acquired by a 1920s Frenchman that is part of the holdings at Lyon's Museum of Natural History but none approaching the scale of Sporry's collection.

The international and domestic clamor for bamboo baskets and other arts prompted the Meiji government, in 1902, to establish a system of schools for teaching traditional Japanese crafts. The Beppu Occupational School continues operating today and provides a one-year program in bamboo basket-making fundamentals. Typically, classes contain 25 to 30 students. The best five students from the first year are selected for a second year of more advanced study. Many of the artists in this exhibit attended the school.

A large number of contemporary Westerners were introduced to Japanese art with the American occupation following World War II. During this time, Lloyd Cotsen, the former CEO of the Neutrogena Corporation, was stationed in Japan and developed an appreciation of Japanese culture. His interest bloomed over the years and eventually resulted in a collection of over 600 bamboo baskets, which he recently donated to the Asian Art Museum in San Francisco. Cotsen purchased his first basket in 1960 at Joseph Cook's newly opened Kuromatsu shop in San Francisco. A captain in the army in the 1950s, Cook was based in Japan when he began purchasing Japanese furniture and decorative arts, including bamboo baskets plucked from junk shops and hardware stores. Cotsen's first acquisition at Kuromatsu was unsigned and so asymmetrical that people often asked if it was broken.

For many years Cook was the main source of Cotsen's bamboo baskets and one

of the reasons for his trips to San Francisco. Then, in the mid-1970s Cotsen met Mary Hunt Kahlenberg, the curator of textiles and costumes at the Los Angeles County Museum of Art, and loaned her several Japanese bamboo baskets for an exhibition she was curating of international objects made of grass. Other important lenders to the show, which traveled to Houston and New York, were Nancy and Dick Bloch.

An increasing number of galleries began representing Japanese bamboo. One of the most significant young dealers was Jeffrey Kleine of Kagedo in Seattle who became interested in bamboo baskets in 1963 as a foreign exchange student. He first offered mostly signed bamboo baskets in 1969 to collectors in the Pacific Northwest. Through the '70s, the number of American collectors enlarged as higher quality Japanese bamboo art became more available in this country. In 1985, Bill Caskey produced his first fair focusing on non-Western arts, including Japanese work, and this exposed a larger audience to new genres.

A major milestone took place in 1988, when the Museum of Cultural History at the University of California at Los Angeles presented *Containing Beauty*, the first exhibition in the United States of Japanese bamboo art and a showcase for pieces, more than half of which were unsigned, available in the United States over the past three decades. Toshiko M. McCallum and Jung-yu S. Lien curated this groundbreaking show, which featured some of the 80 pieces given to the museum by Nancy and Richard Bloch. Other key lenders were Lloyd Cotsen and Helen and Robert Kuhn. To accompany the exhibition, the museum published the first book in the West on Japanese bamboo art, including a history of the role of tea ceremony and interviews with Iizuka Shokansai, Ikeda Hyoa, Tanabe Chikuunsai

III, and Hayakawa Shokosai V. Like the Sporry collection a century before, many of the most important artists were not represented in the show because Americans did not have access to their work.

In 1994, awareness of bamboo art was further advanced by an exhibition at the Smithsonian's Sackler Gallery in Washington D.C. that traveled extensively around the United States. *A Basketmaker in Rural Japan* highlighted the work of Hiroshima Kazuo, a green bamboo utilitarian basket maker. The show was memorable for its large array of objects made for day-to-day life, executed with a multitude of stunning techniques. Sackler curator Louise Cort and Nakamura Kenji published a companion book, still in print, which beautifully captures the heart and mind of a traditional artisan and indirectly provides insight into the lives of all bamboo artists.

In 1997, Mr. Cotsen asked me to look for bamboo baskets during business trips to Japan. Given the size, quality, and scope of his existing collection, I wondered how I might find any artworks of importance. Through introductions, I met several prominent tea ceremony dealers and antique dealers and was able to enrich his holdings. Then I met Sekijima Hisako, a Tokyo artist, who introduced me to Katsushiro Soho, a bamboo craftsman she deeply admired. Katsushiro lives two hours north of Tokyo on his family farm. I was overwhelmed by his originality and I showed photos of the work to Mr. Cotsen, who purchased a magnificent basket. This experience fueled my desire to locate other living bamboo artists in Japan, which led

to visits to bamboo artists on Cotsen's behalf all over Japan.

Two years later a second crucial show, *Bamboo Masterworks*, was organized by the Asia Society of New York. Curated by Kahlenberg, and exhibited in San Francisco, Aspen, Chicago, Los Angeles, and Honolulu, the show was drawn from Cotsen's extensive collection and sparked widespread interest in Japanese bamboo. Simultaneously Cotsen asked Kahlenberg to produce a book on his collection. *Japanese Bamboo Baskets: Masterworks of Form and Texture* greatly expanded information available in the West on Japanese bamboo art and increased public appreciation of the work.

Around this time Fujinuma Noboru asked if TAI Gallery would consider representing his work in the United States. He explained that with the implosion of the Japanese bubble economy it had become increasingly difficult for him to make a living. The focus of the gallery my wife, Mary Hunt Kahlenberg, founded in 1978 was antique textiles, mainly from Indonesia and Japan. When I became involved, the gallery began exhibiting at art fairs in major cities in order to reach a broader public audience. We were always looking for three-dimensional objects to show with textiles and found them in contemporary Japanese bamboo art.

The addition of bamboo art in our gallery attracted a new group of collectors and museums, in the U.S. and the United Kingdom, that were in the process of forming collections. The gallery began to sponsor group and solo exhibitions that brought bamboo artists for visits to the United States. This was a revelatory

experience for the artists. Many had never considered the possibility of traveling outside of Japan. Visiting the homes of people who collected their artwork both delighted and surprised them. Because of the Japanese sense of privacy and the intimate size of their homes, this practice would rarely take place in Japan. The artists were stunned to see traditional vessels and contemporary sculptural pieces displayed side by side. Most Westerners do not arrange flowers in their bamboo baskets but when the artists saw the few who did, it brought them great joy.

During public openings, the frankness of visitors' comments about their baskets was at once shocking and exhilarating. Japanese people do not speak directly about an artist's work so artists never know whether or not their work is well received. This is compounded by the Japanese tendency to place more weight on awards, exhibitions, and titles than their own aesthetic responses. Understanding that his acceptance in the West was rooted in public's love of his baskets, Hayakawa Shokosai V once said that the appreciation of Western collectors meant as much to him as the supreme recognition of being named Living National Treasure of Japan.

For virtually all of these artists, Americans' enthusiasm about their work engenders mixed feelings. The fact that bamboo art is not taken seriously in Japan causes them great unhappiness. On the other hand, they are thankful for the opportunity to explore fresh artistic themes and earn a better living doing the work they love. For the older generation, the future for Japanese bamboo art seems a little brighter.

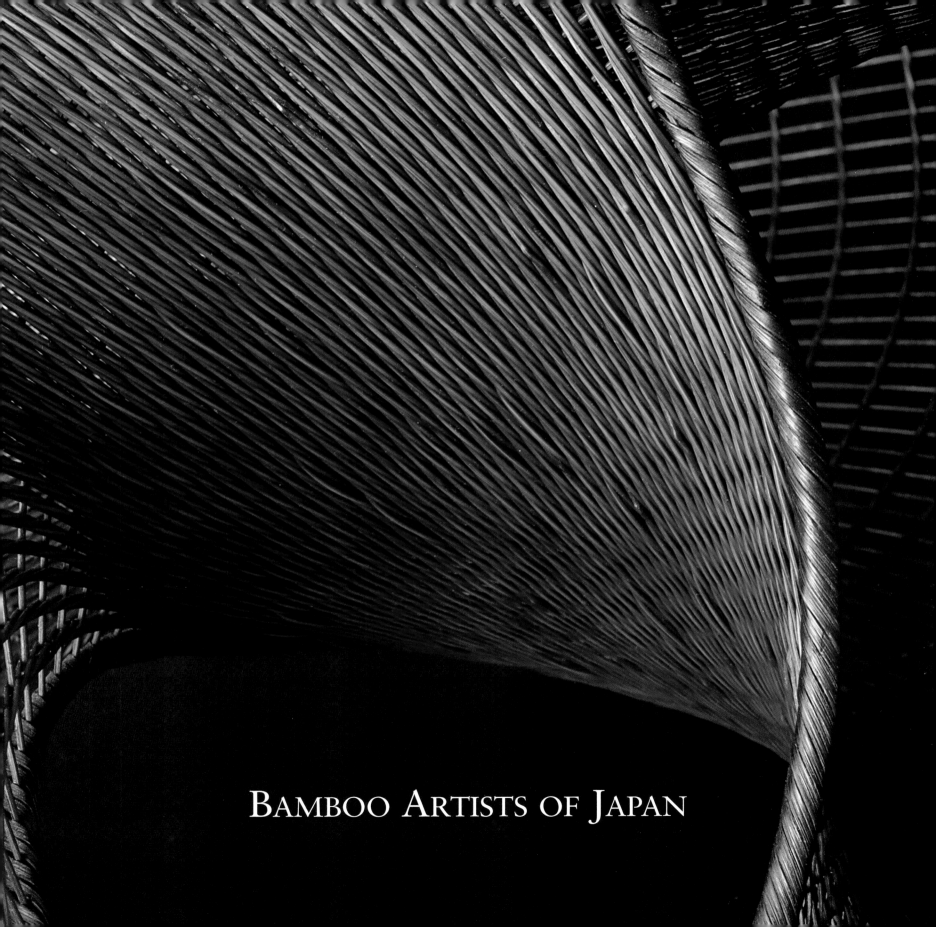

BAMBOO ARTISTS OF JAPAN

MONDEN KOGYOKU (B. 1916)

SPRING RAIN IN MAY, 1975
madake
18 x 21 (diam.) inches
The Buchbinder Family Collection

detail

detail

HIGASHI TAKESONOSAI (1915–2003)

COCONUT, 1984
dyed madake and rattan
7.75 x 22 x 17.5 inches
The Buchbinder Family Collection

MAEDA CHIKUBOSAI II

(1917–2003)

TWIST PATTERN, late Showa Period
madake and rattan
10.5 x 6.5 (diam.) inches
Collection of Matthew and
Carolyn Swartz Bucksbaum

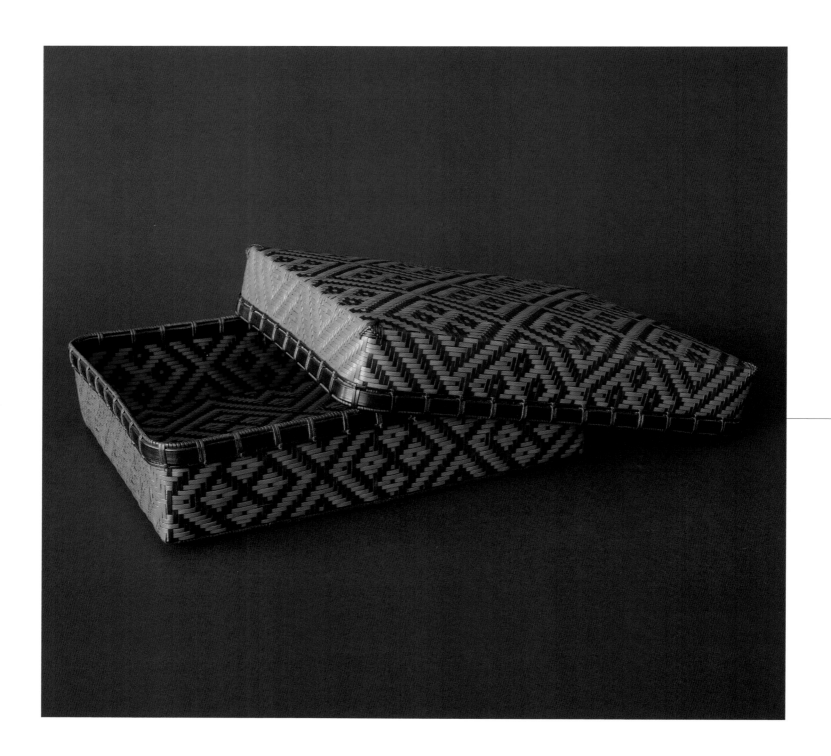

detail

WATANABE SHOCHIKUSAI II (B. 1927)

PAPER BOX, 2001
madake and rattan
3.5 x 13.5 x 10.5 inches
Collection of Marjorie R. and William J. Salman

IIDA SEISEKI (B. 1929)

CORN PATTERN BAMBOO BASKET 1994
madake and rattan
9.5 x 17.25 inches
Collection of Walter and Celia Gilbert

detail

detail

HATAKEYAMA SEIDO (B. 1930)

FLOWER BASKET, 2003
madake and rattan
9.5 x 16 (diam.) inches
Collection of John and Mary Louise Bailey

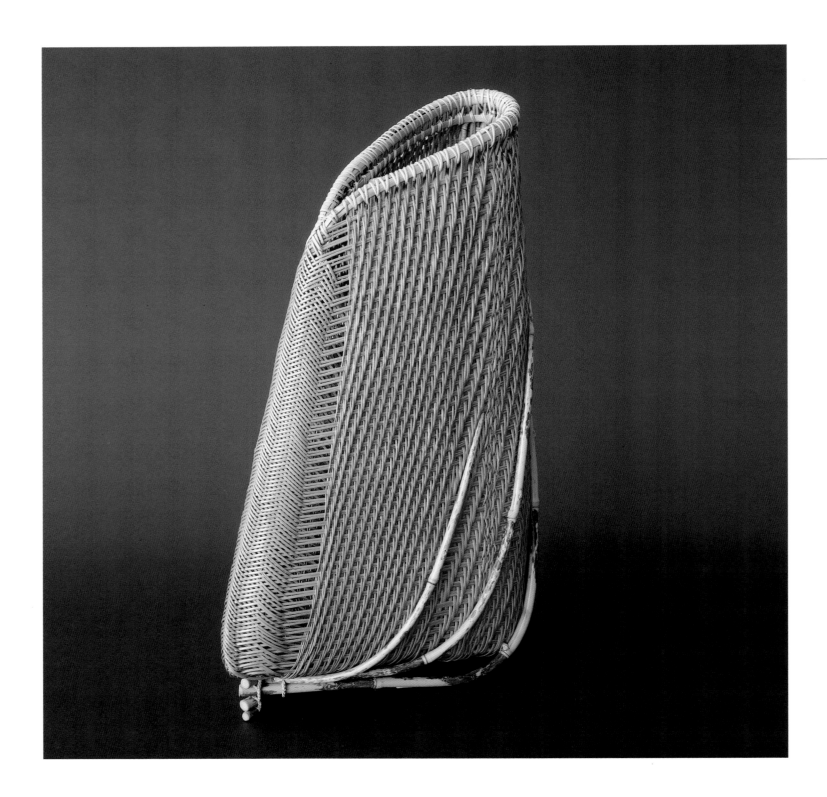

detail

HONMA KAZUAKI (B. 1930)

ORIGIN IV, 1996
madake, menyadake and rattan
26 x 14 x 7.5 inches
Collection of Diane and Arthur Abbey

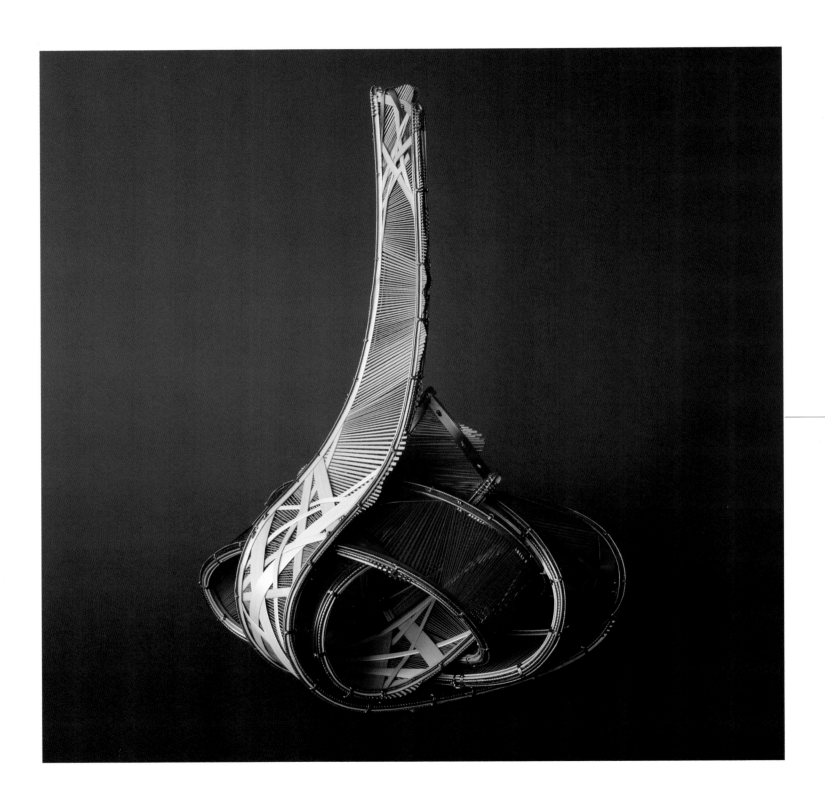

detail

TORII IPPO (B. 1930)

DEVELOPMENT–PIERCING, 2002
madake and rattan
29 x 22 x 17 inches
The Buchbinder Family Collection

SUGITA JOZAN (B. 1932)

BUDDING, 2001
madake and rattan
11.5 x 12 (diam.) inches
Collection of Diane and Arthur Abbey

detail

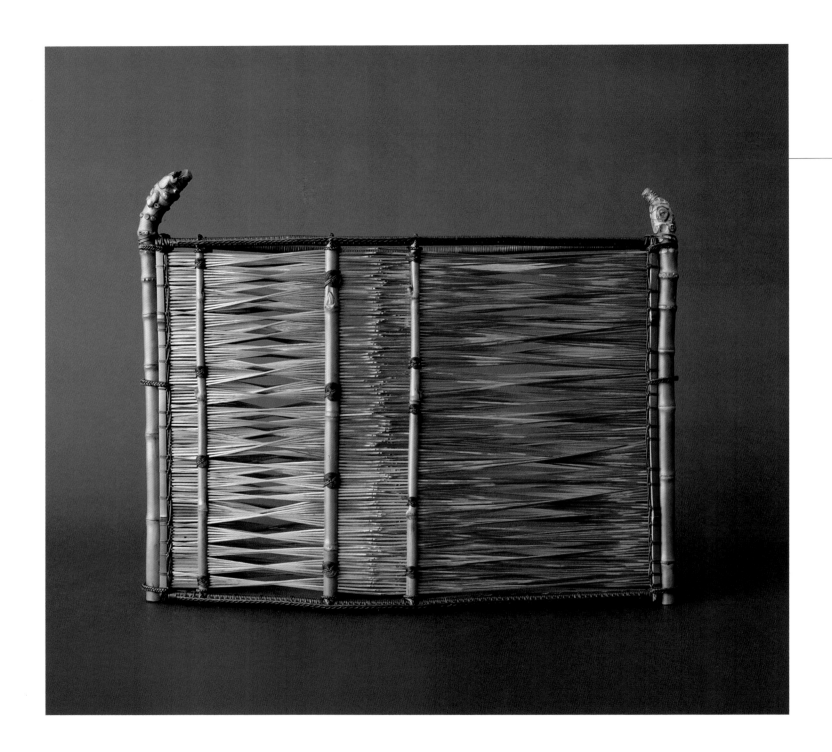

detail

KOSUGE HOUNSAI KOGETSU

(B. 1932)

LAKE REFLECTIONS, 2004

hobichiku, susudake and rattan,
tube made out of Edo period susudake

20.5 x 25 x 5.5 inches

Courtesy of Lloyd and Margit Cotsen
Reproduced from the collection of, and
with the permission of Lloyd E. Cotsen.

HAYAKAWA SHOKOSAI V

(B. 1932)

OVERLAID DIAMOND PATTERN
FLOWER BASKET, 2002
madake and rattan
12.75 x 10.25 (diam.) inches
Private Collection

detail

KATSUSHIRO SOHO (B. 1934)

PLAYFUL, 2002
nemagari
13.5 x 15 (diam.) inches
Collection of Lolli Thurm

MINOURA CHIKUHO (B. 1934)

DEW DROP, 2004
madake and rattan
22.5 x 21 x 11.5 inches
Collection of Matthew and
Carolyn Swartz Bucksbaum

detail

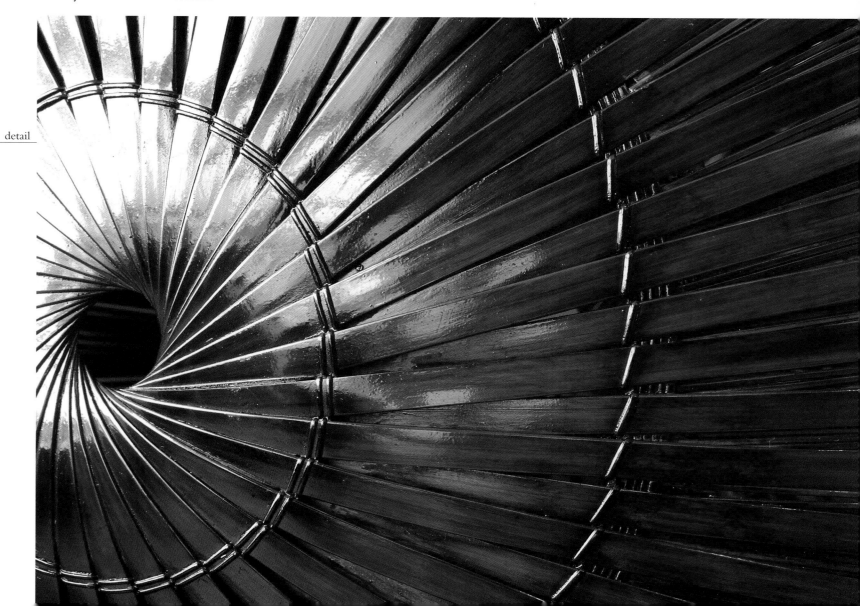

detail

KAJIWARA KOHO (B. 1935)

AUTUMN COLOR, 2000
madake, hobichiku, and rattan
13 x 9 (diam.) inches
Collection of Barbara Billings and Ernest Vogel

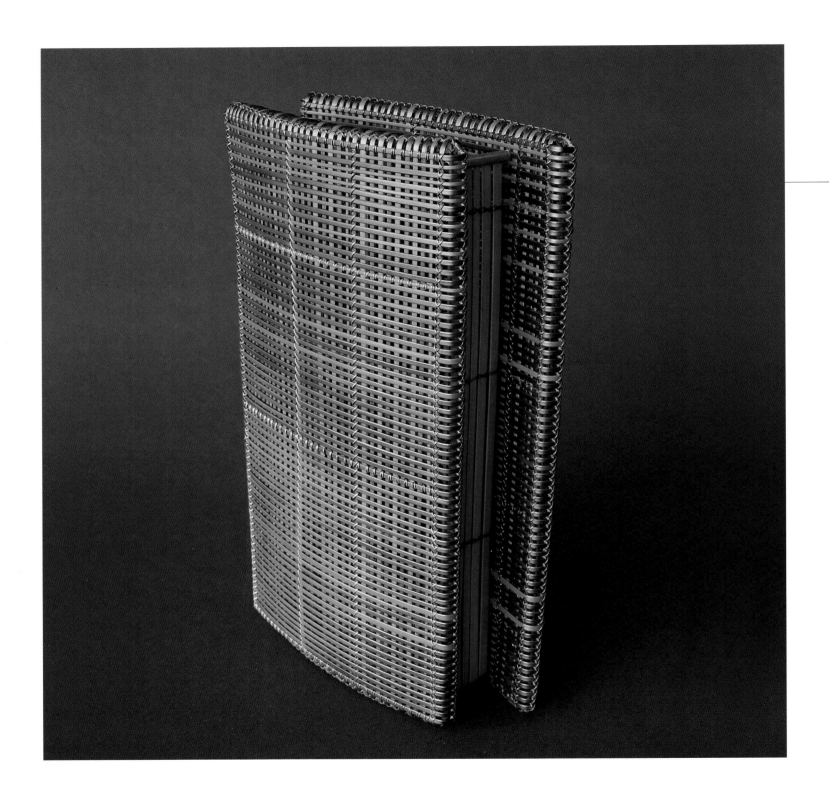

detail

YAKO HODO (B. 1940)

CITY LIGHT, 2000
madake and rattan
13.75 x 8.5 x 3.75 inches
Collection of Ritalou and Robert Harris

detail

YAMAGUCHI RYUUN (B. 1940)

CRASHING WAVE, 2001
bamboo and rattan
18 x 24 x 18 inches
Collection of Matthew and
Carolyn Swartz Bucksbaum

KAJIWARA AYA (B. 1941)

SPIRAL PATTERN FLOWER BASKET, 2004
madake and rattan
8.5 x 12 (diam.) inches
Collection of Bradley Gordon, in memory of Angelique Leibow

detail

detail

YUFU SHOHAKU (B. 1941)

SACRED LILY, 2004
madake and bamboo roots
20 x 22 (diam.) inches
The Buchbinder Family Collection

ABE KIRAKU MOTOSHI (B. 1942)

OCEAN CURRENT, 2000
madake and rattan
8 x 12.5 (diam.) inches
Collection of Eugenie and Lael Johnson

detail

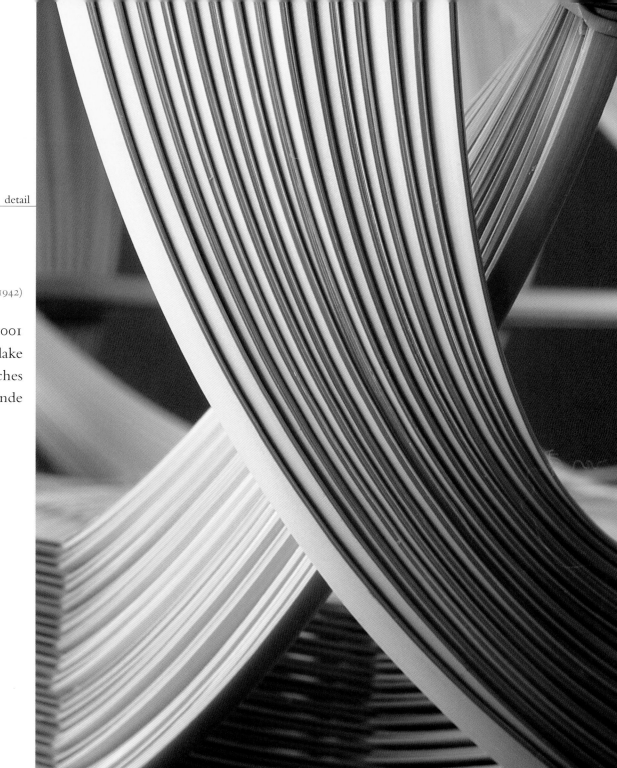

detail

SHONO TOKUZO (B. 1942)

WAVES OF SWAYING RICE PLANTS, 2001
madake
12.5 x 21 (diam.) inches
Collection of Eric and Karen Ende

MONDEN YUICHI (B. 1942)

BORN, 2003
madake
18 x 9.5 x 10.5 inches
Museum of Arts and Design, New York
Museum purchase with funds provided by the Collections Committee, 2003

detail

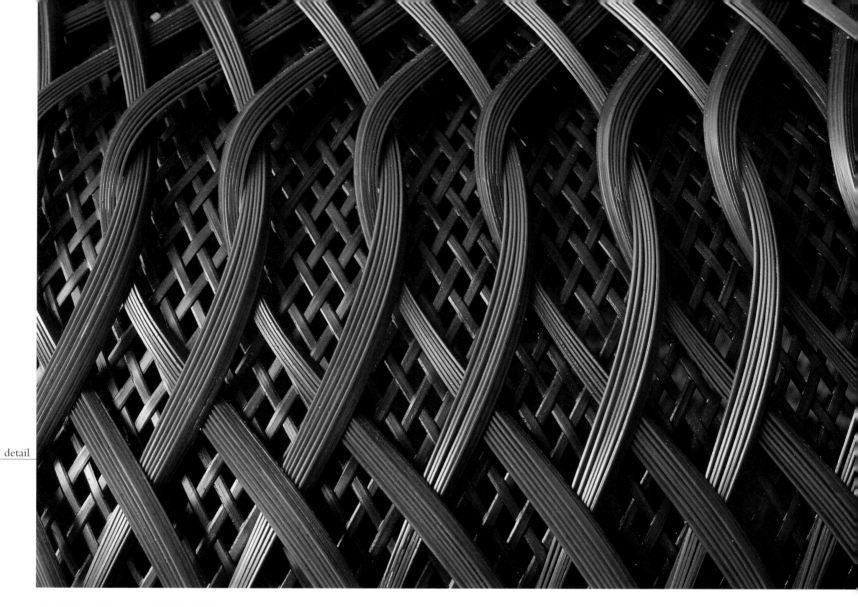

detail

FUJINUMA NOBORU (B. 1945)

ADORNED HEART, 2004
madake and rattan
10 x 15.5 x 14.5 inches
Collection of the late Myron Szold and Pamela Crutchfield

TANAKA KYOKUSHO (B. 1947)

AJIRO PLAITING IN CONTRASTING COLORS, 1993
madake and rattan
6 x 13.5 x 11 inches
Collection of Matthew and Carolyn Swartz Bucksbaum

detail

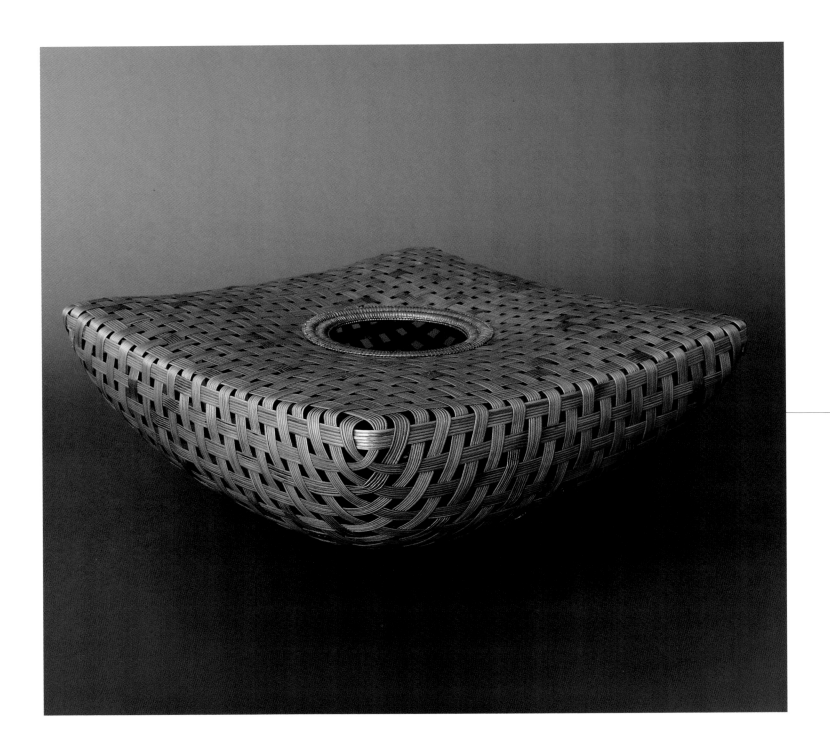

detail

TANIOKA AIKO (B. 1947)

MOTHER EARTH, 2003
madake and rattan
7 x 16.5 x 16.5 inches
Collection of Bradley Gordon, in memory of Angelique Leibow

UENO MASAO (B. 1949)

ROTATION OF ELLIPSE MAKES TWO
TRANSPARENT DRUMS, 2004
madake, rattan, urushi, and gold leaf
20 x 20 (diam.) inches
The Ruth & Sherman Lee Institute for
Japanese Art at the Clark Center

detail

FUJITSUKA SHOSEI (B. 1949)

UNTITLED, 2004
madake and rattan
12 x 17 (diam.) inches
Collection of Eugenie and Lael Johnson

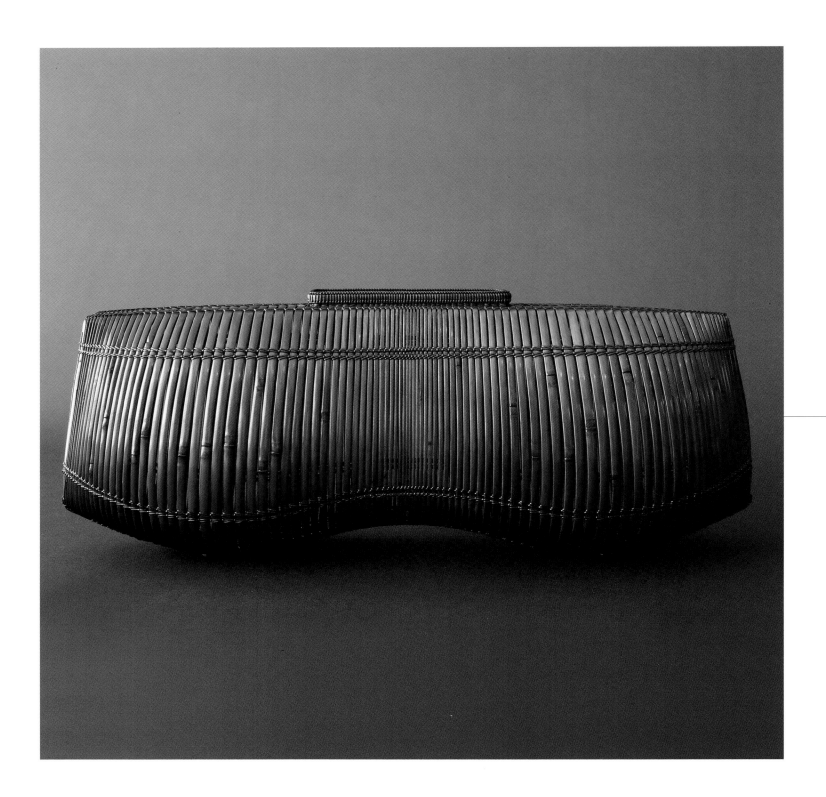

TANIOKA SHIGEO (B. 1949)

ALL ENCOMPASSING, 2002
susudake (smoked aged bamboo)
8.5 x 20.5 x 5.5 inches
Courtesy of Lloyd and Margit Cotsen
Reproduced from the collection of, and with the permission of Lloyd E. Cotsen.

detail

detail

HONDA SYORYU (B. 1951)

DANCE, 2000
madake and rattan
19 x 21 x 21 inches
Courtesy of Lloyd and Margit Cotsen
Reproduced from the collection of, and
with the permission of Lloyd E. Cotsen.

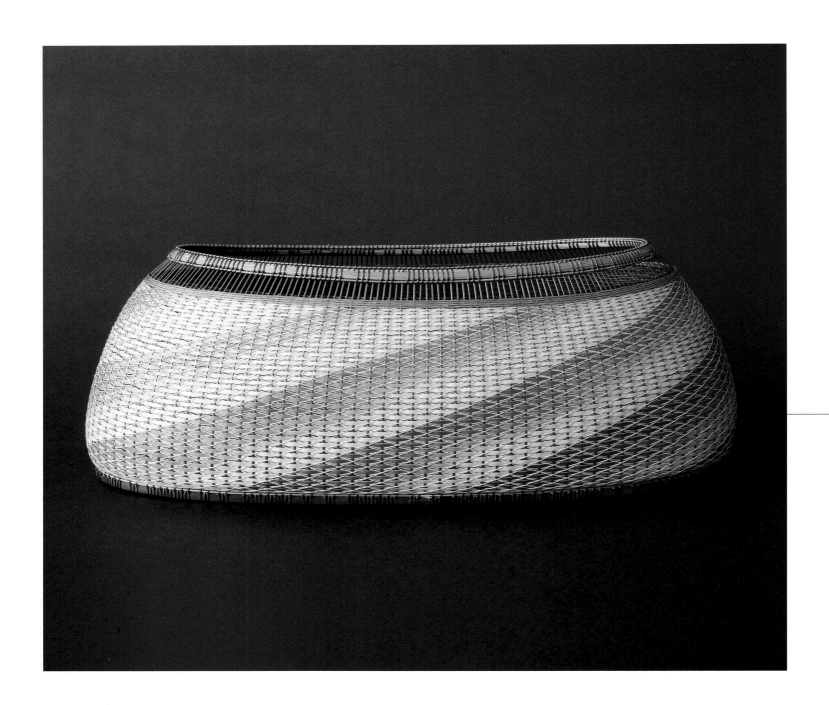

KIBE SEIHO (B. 1951)

MOUNTAIN RANGE, 2001
madake and rattan
6.375 x 17.5 x 7 inches
Collection of the late Myron Szold and Pamela Crutchfield

detail

detail

NAGAKURA KENICHI (B. 1952)

BAMBOO VASTNESS, 2005

madake

11 x 29.5 x 18.5 inches

Collection of the late Myron Szold and Pamela Crutchfield

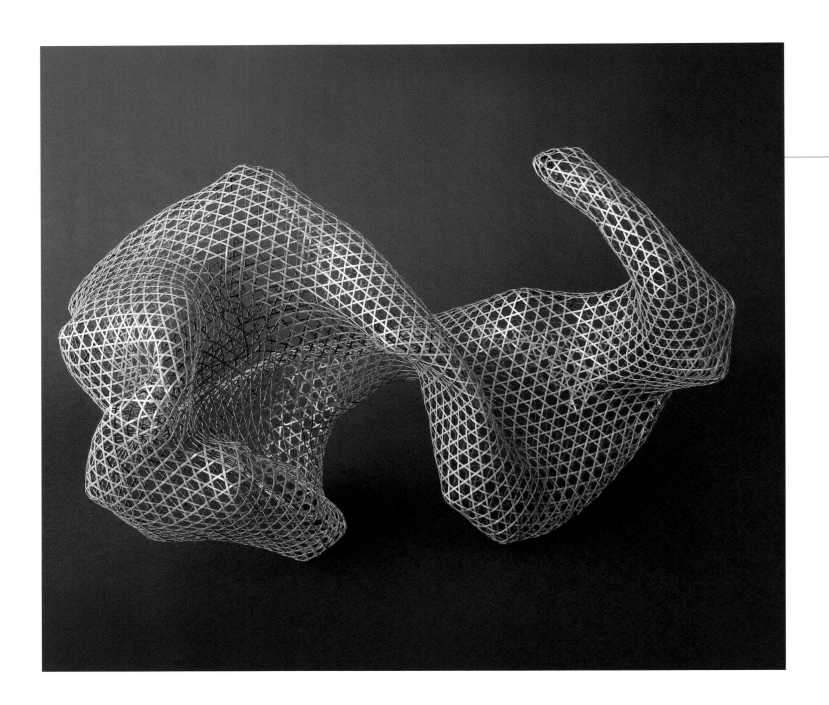

detail

MORIGAMI JIN (B. 1955)

KIRIN, 2005
madake
13.5 x 20.5 x 12 inches
Private Collection

detail

KAWANO SHOKO (B. 1957)

BIRTH, 2003
madake and rattan
11 x 14 (diam.) inches
Collection of the late Myron Szold and Pamela Crutchfield

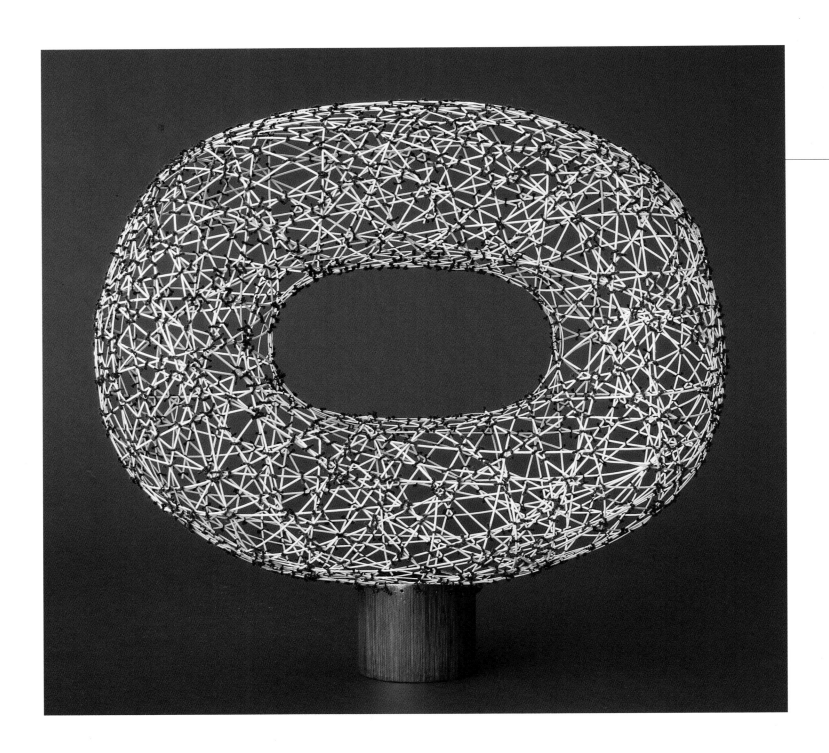

KAWASHIMA SHIGEO (B. 1958)

COSMIC RING, 2001
madake and cotton threads
14 x 14.5 x 5 inches
Courtesy of Lloyd and Margit Cotsen
Reproduced from the collection of,
and with the permission of Lloyd E. Cotsen.

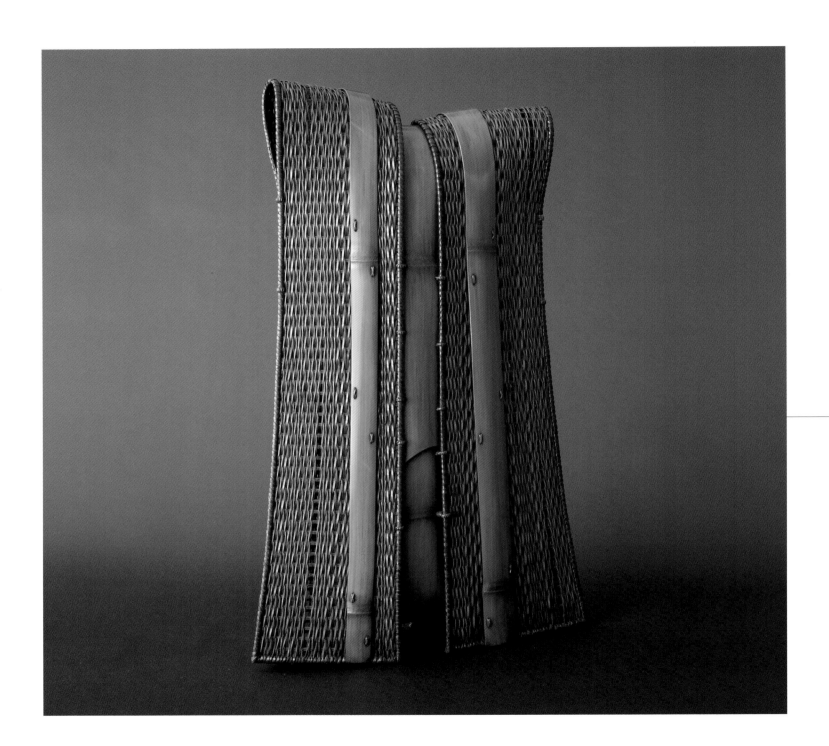

detail

HONMA HIDEAKI (B. 1959)

PROFOUND, 2000

madake and menyadake

33 x 20 x 5.5 inches

Clark Family Collection, on long-term loan to
The Ruth & Sherman Lee Institute for Japanese Art

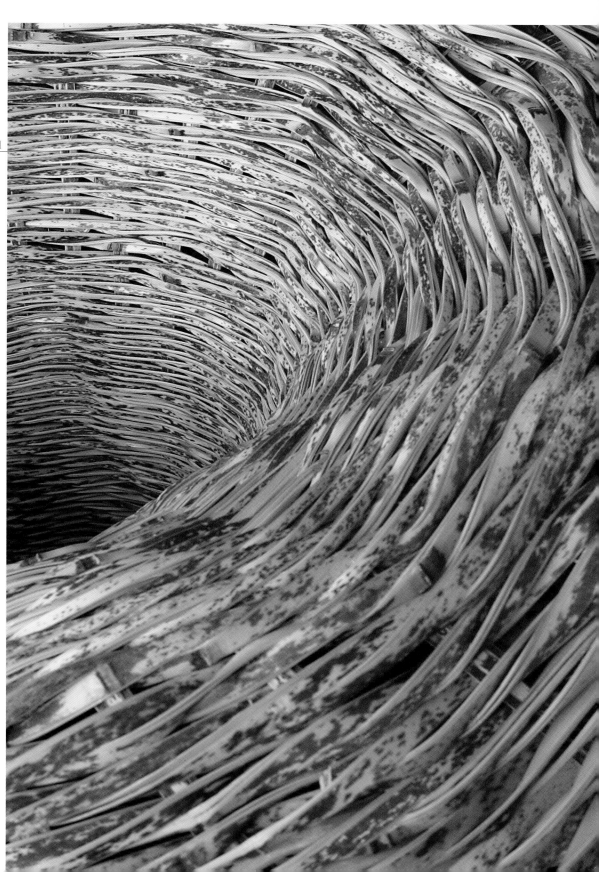

detail

TANABE SHOCHIKU III (B. 1973)

CONNECTION–CLOUD, 2003
torachiku (tiger bamboo)
18 x 22 x 20 inches
Collection of Marjorie R. and
William J. Salman

detail

MIMURA CHIKUHO (B. 1973)

CLOUD ON THE PEAK, 2005
madake
6.5 x 14 x 13.5 inches
Collection of Barbara Billings and Ernest Vogel

detail

NAKATOMI HAJIME (B. 1974)

FRAGRANT WIND, 2004
madake and rattan
14 x 8.5 (diam.) inches
Collection of Betsy and Edward Cohen

ARTISTS' BIOGRAPHIES

(ARTISTS ARE LISTED ALPHABETICALLY BY FAMILY NAME)

Abe Kiraku Motoshi (b. 1942) p.52–53

Abe's career as a bamboo artist began auspiciously. Right out of high school, he studied with Shono Shounsai, Japan's first Living National Treasure in bamboo arts.

"My apprenticeship to master Shounsai was a very difficult two years," Abe recalls. "He was so great an artist that I felt I was inferior. It took me well over 10 years to get over those feelings. I realized, after all, I can only be myself. Nothing more, nothing less. My master said to me before passing away in 1974, 'It takes a lot of patience to craft bamboo, so you need a wife with lots of patience.' He said this as he introduced me to the woman who was to become my wife. I owe him a great debt."

In 1967, Abe inherited his father's bamboo basket business. Less than a decade later, he was admitted to the Japan Traditional Craft Arts Exhibition and became a full member by 1980. He has won numerous prizes and served as a judge for important regional shows. His work is part of the permanent collections of the Beppu City Museum, the city where he was born, and has been exhibited at the National Museum of Modern Art, Tokyo and the Asian Art Museum of San Francisco.

Fujinuma Noboru (b. 1945) p.58–59

Fujinuma Noboru's early interests were photography and engineering. At 27, he traveled to Paris and returned home intent on studying traditional Japanese arts. Shortly thereafter, he quit his job at Nikon to apprentice with the respected bamboo basket maker Yagisawa Keizo.

For half-a-dozen years, he struggled to execute his design ideas because he lacked confidence in his technique. This changed by 1992 when, his reputation growing, he received the Tokyo Governor's Prize at the 39th Traditional Craft Arts Exhibition. His winning piece was purchased by the National Museum of Modern Art, Tokyo.

"What is art? What is the criteria for art?" he muses. "Not many people in Japan can answer this question clearly. For me, art is not just about the surface. It's something invisible that speaks to the viewer."

A finalist for the Cotsen Bamboo Prize in 2000, Fujinuma plays tennis, studies English, and works in his garden at home near Tokyo. In addition to exhibitions of his work in numerous art museums, Fujinuma was featured in a solo show in 2005 at the Japanese American Cultural and Community Center in Los Angeles. His pieces are part of collections at the Ruth and Sherman Lee Institute for Japanese Art at the Clark Center in Hanford, California and the Denver Art Museum.

Fujitsuka Shosei (b. 1949) p.66–67

Fujitsuka's range is broad, from typical basket and vessel forms to abstract sculptures inspired by nature. Because his pieces defy neat categorization, he was for decades rejected for exhibitions in Japan. However he persisted in making the risky aesthetic choices that have won him the freedom to express his distinctive voice.

"People involved in the traditional craft group in Japan are working more on technique," he notes, "but design is more interesting to me."

After graduation from high school, Fujitsuka worked for a record producer and for a company that serviced optical equipment. The rigid corporate environment didn't suit him; he longed for the opportunity to work for himself and the time to pursue astronomy, an avocation that continues to absorb him today.

In 1972, inspired by items in a bamboo shop window, he began an apprenticeship with Baba Shodo. For more than two decades he earned his living making bamboo lampshades until his work was rewarded with a Superior Prize at the Traditional Craft Arts Exhibition.

Fujitsuka has been honored with television appearances, prizes, and solo and group exhibitions in Asia, Europe, and the United States. His work is in the collections of the Japanese Agency for Cultural Affairs and the Japan Foundation.

Hatakeyama Seido (b. 1930) p.26–27

Until American collectors discovered his work, Hatakeyama supported himself by making bamboo souvenirs for tourists. For a time he ran a successful business, with over a dozen employees, crafting bamboo brooches. While he focused on commercial work, he made sculptures for his own pleasure and, eventually, for display at the Traditional Japan Craft Arts Exhibition.

Hatakeyama had a childhood accident that impaired the use of his right leg. When he was a teenager, an instructor at a vocational school encouraged him to learn bamboo. Later he apprenticed to leading bamboo master Kosuge Shochikudo in his hometown of Sado. Through the 1950s he was swept along by the movement to create sculpture with bamboo and won his first prize, in 1959, at a local exhibition.

A superb technician, the artist's signature is *tabane* plaiting and *masawari*, a challenging technique of knotting pliant strips of bamboo that have been cut from the flesh of the plant.

Hatakeyama has exhibited at Kanai Town Hall Gallery and the Setsuryosha Art Museum in Niigata, Japan.

Hayakawa Shokosai V (b. 1932) p.36–37

According to Japanese custom, only one son of each generation is permitted to inherit the family tradition. Forty-eight years ago, Hayakawa Shokosai V was chosen by his father to learn the craft. The artist is the fifth-generation descendant of Shokosai I, who was the first bamboo artist to sign his work.

In 2003, Shokosai V was named a Living National Treasure in bamboo arts. Two years later, he received the Order of the Rising Sun from the Japanese government. His work is housed at Tokyo's National Museum of Modern Art, the Agency for Cultural Affairs, Asian Art Museum of San Francisco, Denver Art Museum, and Ise Shrine, the state guesthouse in Kyoto where visiting dignitaries reside.

Of his work with bamboo, Hayakawa says, "Let me tell you the truth. I was not at first fond of this art. I did not consider myself skilled enough. But I could not stand the idea of terminating the artist line of our family. After five or six years of hard training, I made my first bamboo basket. The excitement of creating it was unforgettable."

"I realized that the work is really a reflection of inner self. If you try to over-manipulate bamboo to make a shape, the shape becomes unnatural or even breaks by force. I began to realize that just as we have feelings, so does bamboo. I constantly talk and listen to it now."

Higashi Takesonosai (1915–2003)   p.18–19

"A writer uses words to create magic," Higashi once said. "I use bamboo."

Born in Kyoto and apprenticing to Kaneko Chikkosai in 1931, the artist's speciality is basket making with an architectural flavor. His work incorporates *susudake*, or smoked bamboo from the rafters of farm houses over 150 years old, non-plaited techniques, and other inventions of his own.

Prolifically honored, with entrance into Nitten 28 times and full membership in the Japan Craft Arts Association in 1994, Higashi won the Prince Takamatsu Commemorative Prize in 1995 and had numerous solo exhibitions throughout Japan. In 2002, Lloyd Cotsen and Robert Coffland published a book on his life and artistic career.

When asked, at the age of 83, about his continuing commitment to bamboo, he noted that his vision of what he wanted to say in his art had grown stronger as he grew older.

"A great work is a combination of artistic beauty and technical excellence, but a masterpiece adds another quality that is a reflection of you as a person," he said. "My goal as an artist is to leave such pieces when I leave this world."

Honda Syoryu (b. 1951)   p.70–71

Honda began his career studying bamboo basket making for flower arranging but the limitations of this centuries-old genre constrained his creativity. An innovator, he crafts dramatic, undulating sculpture that demonstrates his fascination with line, volume, and space. Seamless lengths of braided bamboo, dyed in warm shades of tobacco, gold, and bronze, resemble leather or metal. The artist is a master at tight *ajiro* plaiting, a technique he has adapted from generations of Japanese bamboo box makers.

For years his artistic career came to a halt because of the lack of interest in bamboo artists among Japanese collectors. To earn a living, he worked long hours, seven days a week, filling wholesale orders for simple bamboo flower baskets. Recently, after many rejections from Japan's bamboo establishment, Honda has begun to achieve recognition in his home country and in the West.

A finalist for the Cotsen Bamboo Prize in 2000, 2002, and 2004, Honda's work is now part of the permanent collections of the Museum of Arts and Design in New York City, Asian Art Museum of San Francisco, Boston Museum of Fine Arts, Mint Museum of Craft and Design, and the Ruth and Sherman Lee Institute for Japanese Art at the Clark Center.

Honma Hideaki (b. 1959)   p.82–83

As a young man, Honma was a soldier in the Japanese air force. After an accident caused a loss of sight in one eye, he was forced to resign. His uncle and adopted father, the esteemed bamboo artist Honma Kazuaki, had no heir so Honma, who loved to draw and work with his hands, stepped in to carry on the family's bamboo business.

On his native Sado Island, Honma is inspired by the abundant natural beauty. Bamboo provides a vehicle for expressing his passion and appreciation for the plants and animals that surround him in his daily life. He uses *menya*, a type of soft, pliable bamboo that only grows on the island.

In addition to practicing karate and tea ceremony, Honma balances his devotion to his family with a commitment to community, spending much of his time as an advocate of local culture. Recently he has re-dedicated himself to developing his distinctive style, separate from his well-known father.

His work is included in the collection of the Ruth and Sherman Lee Institute for Japanese Art.

Honma Kazuaki (b. 1930)   p.28–29

In 1952, Honma apprenticed to the great 20th-century bamboo artist, Hayashi Shogetsusai. Within a year, his career as a professional artist was launched with an important local award. But long days making exhibition artwork and flower baskets to support his family cost him his health and Honma decided to concentrate on commercial work. At the height of his success he employed 50 assistants to make intricate and highly coveted bamboo brooches.

Once financially secure, he devoted himself to his art, winning important prizes and leadership posts. He moved beyond sculpture and flower baskets to create a series of bamboo paintings that earned him the two Toksen prizes necessary to become a full member of Japan's Nitten world. Honma is the only living bamboo artist to achieve this status and has used his position to encourage other bamboo artists to expand their vision.

Now in his fifth decade as an artist, Honma's signature is his use of *hobichiku*, a round sooted bamboo suited for his rhythmically curved sculptures. He has published a book, *The Shapes in Bamboo*, and been featured in numerous exhibitions, including a solo show in Washington, D.C. sponsored by the Japanese Embassy. His work is in the permanent collection of the Asian Art Museum of San Francisco.

Iida Seiseki (b. 1929)   p.24–25

After World War II Iida was walking in the countryside contemplating the devastation and misery that the war had caused. He decided to commit his life to bringing more beauty into the world.

He approached Iizuka Rokansai, one of the most prestigious bamboo artists in the world, and asked to become his apprentice. Iizuka would not even speak to him until he returned with his father. Ultimately Iizuka took him on, the last student he would ever have.

Iida went to live with him and was assigned menial tasks such as sweeping floors for several years until he was permitted even to touch the bamboo. The great artist gave him the artistic name that means "pure stone."

After Iizuka's death, Iida went out on his own, working as a graphic designer and printer to earn a living and making baskets in his spare time. His platters and vessels, which have received more than a dozen awards over the course of his career, are noted for their meticulous technique and range of contemporary and traditional styles. They are included in the collections of the Tochigi Prefectural Museum of Fine Arts and the Ruth and Sherman Lee Institute for Japanese Art.

Kajiwara Aya (b. 1941)   p.48–49

Kajiwara is the first and only female bamboo artist to become a full member of the Japan Craft Arts Association. She became interested in the genre while helping her husband, Kajiwara Koho, with his work. When her youngest daughter entered grade school, she enrolled at Beppu Occupational School, the premier bamboo arts training institution in the country, and graduated in 1980. Encouraged by her teacher, she and 15 other women formed a bamboo craft association that organized its own exhibitions.

Shortly thereafter she began winning awards for her baskets, including the Beppu Mayor's Award at the 22nd Bamboo Craft Arts New Work Exhibition. She was first admitted to Japan's esteemed Traditional Craft Arts Exhibition in 1992, and thereafter numerous times, and is the recipient of the President's Prize, the highest honor bestowed by this organization.

"Many bamboo artists must take part-time jobs, which keeps us from our craft art work," she says. "You cannot become rich as a bamboo artist even if your work wins awards of excellence. But you know I love working with bamboo. I am still weaving and plaiting in the middle of the night. You cannot create that wonderful curved line with any other materials and the feeling when you have achieved what you imagined is unforgettable."

Kajiwara Koho (b. 1935) p.42-43

Kajiwara Koho was born in a mountain village in Oita Prefecture. He loved drawing and crafts so much that a family friend suggested he study bamboo with Iwao Kounsai. That apprenticeship lasted a decade.

He was first admitted to the Beppu City Art Exhibition in 1965 and to the Japan Traditional Craft Arts Exhibition 14 years later. The association granted him full membership in 1985 and the next year the Ministry of International Trade and Industry recognized him as a Traditional Craft Arts Skill Holder.

Among his many honors are the Oita Asahi Broadcasting Prize at the 40th Japan Traditional Craft Arts Seibu Exhibition and the presentation of his work to the president of France. In 2000, one of his pieces was selected as a special gift of Oita Prefecture to the Emperor of Japan. His baskets are part of the collections at the Asian Art Museum of San Francisco, Beppu Museum of Art, and Oita Prefectural Art Hall.

"A part of my brain," he says, "is constantly thinking about the next work no matter what I am doing. I try to express the natural beauty of Japan through bamboo. If you are the type of person who does not think anything upon seeing a little flower growing along the street, you should forget about becoming an artist."

Katsushiro Soho (b. 1934) p.38-39

Nature is an important theme for Katsushiro, who comes from a farming family and spends his days working the land. The changing seasons spark ideas for his bamboo vessels, which represent the movement of wind across rice fields and shallow water beneath stones.

Katsushiro's father and his first teacher, Kikuchi Yoshii, were also farmers who made bamboo baskets in the months when the fields were fallow. Watching his father carve abstract sculptures in wood and stone gave the young Katsushiro a taste for the artist's life. But the path to that career was not easy. His six-year apprenticeship with Kikuchi included child care and house cleaning. He spent two additional years studying with Yagisawa Keizo and crafting commercial brooches and vases. With the encouragement of his third teacher, Saito Bunseki, he began using bamboo to make art.

Katsushiro's innovative sculptures are included in collections at the National Museum of Modern Art in Tokyo, the Japanese Agency for Cultural Affairs, Tochigi Prefectural Museum of Fine Arts, Asian Art Museum of San Francisco, and the Ruth and Sherman Lee Institute for Japanese Art. In 2005, he became Japan's Living National Treasure in bamboo arts.

"In the beginning I was only making baskets for use, I didn't even think of them as art," he says.

"When I began submitting them in exhibitions I started imagining that these pieces would last forever and that felt very good."

Kawano Shoko (b. 1957) p.78-79

Kawano was a relative newcomer to bamboo, unknown in his country and, at 45, young by Japanese standards, when he won the prestigious Cotsen Prize in 2002.

For years his dream was to become a sculptor but, despite numerous tries, he was unable to pass the entrance exams at the National Art University in Tokyo. One day he came across a basket by the Living National Treasure Shono Shounsai, and was so stunned by its beauty that he applied to the highly competitive Beppu Occupational School to study bamboo. In his first year, he was one of only 25 or 30 students to be accepted. His second year, only five were invited to continue.

Kawano's signature technique is his open twill work, which he has improved primarily through his own determination. His conservative approach to artmaking involves a slow, step-by-step mastery of the intricate skills that are integral to making the highest quality bamboo sculpture.

In 2004, he became a full member of the Traditional Craft Arts Association. His pieces are part of collections at the Asian Art Museum of San Francisco and Mint Museum of Craft and Design.

Kawashima Shigeo (b. 1958) p.80-81

American interest in Kawashima's large, outdoor, site-specific sculpture has been so great that the artist has begun making small-scale models for purchase by private collectors. The creator of contemporary designs executed with fresh-cut bamboo, his sense of adventure is inspired by Shono Shounsei, Japan's first Living National Treasure in bamboo arts, who was a major advocate of the sculptural possibilities of bamboo.

Kawashima was in his twenties when he began teaching at the Beppu Occupational School. Because of his youth, his students did not take him seriously until he challenged them to a competition to see who could split bamboo fastest and most accurately.

In the last decade, he has placed pieces in some 30 public locations throughout Japan, Europe, and the United States, including the Asian Art Museum of San Francisco, and exhibited in a dozen shows featuring emerging contemporary artists. His creativity and quickness to master new techniques have established his reputation as a leader in the next wave of bamboo sculptors.

Kibe Seiho (b. 1951) p.72-73

Bamboo was Kibe's ticket out of a mundane life. He was working as a gas station attendant when, in his thirties, he resolved to find a way to make his life more meaningful. Despite his family's objections, the pressure they exerted on him to

take over operation of their farm, and the fact that making a living in bamboo was extremely difficult, Kibe quit his job to learn the genre.

Though he has no formal art training, the artist's work illustrates an intuitive sense of proportion and an ability to produce complex plaiting that is suggestive of quilting. His baskets exude a quietness that belies his personality, which is gregarious, earthy, and funny.

For many years Kibe has steeped himself in traditional Japanese styles and techniques but recently he has expanded his repertoire, moving strongly into the contemporary realm.

The artist became a full member of the Traditional Craft Arts Association in 2000 and won prestigious prizes at regional and national exhibitions thereafter. In 2004, he was a finalist for the Cotsen Bamboo Prize. Kibe's baskets are in the permanent collection of the Denver Art Museum and the Asian Art Museum of San Francisco .

Kosuge Hounsai Kogetsu (b. 1932) p.34-35

Kosuge is the son of Kosuge Chikudo, a well-known bamboo artist in Sado. As a boy, he spent many hours in his father's studio learning basketry. He was a slow learner and unsure of himself. Often he felt inferior to his father's assistants and students who were quicker studies. At one point he declared, "I am no good. I am quitting," to which his father responded that his son had a wonderful gift. "If you are a fast learner," his father told him, "you are not putting enough effort into it."

Kosuge studied tea ceremony and created baskets that expressed his earnest, charismatic personality. Among his prestigious awards are the Minister of Economy, Trade and Industry Prize at Japan's Flower and Tea Ware Art Exhibition and the Niigata Nippo Prize at the 16th Prefectural Art Exhibition. In 1972, the Niigata Governor commissioned the artist to create a basket as a gift to the Emperor of Japan and six years later he became a full member of the Traditional Craft Art Association.

Despite this recognition, in the 1970s he rejected Japan's rigid system of public exhibitions in favor of working for himself. He became independent to focus on making baskets that would please tea masters and his clients.

Kosuge's work is in the collection of the Asian Art Museum of San Francisco.

Maeda Chikubosai II (1917–2003) p.20-21

Maeda's father, Maeda Chikubosai I, was pivotal in promoting individual expression in the bamboo arts. His son was born late and didn't receive his father's attention right away. He learned bamboo from his father's students. Finally, in 1945, after proving his sincerity to his work, he submitted to the Osaka Craft Exhibition. He won eight subsequent awards.

In 1952 he succeeded to the Chikubosai name and set out in a new direction, creating his own style that involved weaving extremely fine strips of bamboo into ingenious and eccentric forms. After seeking advice from Iizuka Rokansai, his work was accepted in Nitten in 1953 and twelve times thereafter. That same year, one of his baskets was presented to the Emperor as a gift from the governor of Osaka. His work has been part of numerous traveling exhibitions in Germany, New Zealand, and Austria and part of the 1979 "Japan Style" exhibit in England. Maeda's work is part of the Asian Art Museum of San Francisco and Denver Art Museum collections.

Maeda received the Order of Cultural Merit from the Japanese government in 1992 and the supreme honor, in 1995, of becoming the third bamboo artist designated a Living National Treasure.

"I sometimes find myself wondering if the best piece I make will be my last or even if I have made it already," he once said. "Bragging about your work is not good. An artist needs humility to make great art."

Mimura Chikuho (b. 1973)   p.86–87
Mimura's career is still young. He began with ambitions to become a classical trombonist but returned from conservatory in Germany with an interest in working with his hands. He took a part-time job as a gardener and made bamboo fences before returning to his studies, this time at the Beppu Occupational School. There, he founded an association of young bamboo artists.

After graduation, he apprenticed with a Beppu craftsman, Yufu Shohaku, who taught him a traditional, rustic style of basketry that incorporates roots and whole chunks of bamboo. Mimura has used that technique to create his own, contemporary form of sculptural vessels.

An independent artist, Mimura has chosen to sidestep Japan's public exhibition system in favor of working on his own. He has demonstrated basket making for public audiences in Los Angeles, Santa Fe, San Francisco, and Naples, Florida, and was included in *The Next Generation* exhibit at the University of Arkansas.

Minoura Chikuho (b. 1934)   p.40–41
"Bamboo has a certain tenderness, a breathing quality," Minoura has said. "When you weave it and pattern it, light passes through it; it is transparent and solid at the same time. It also retains the qualities it has in nature—flexibility and strength."

Minoura, who was selected by the city of Sasayama as an Intangible Cultural Asset in 1985, began studying bamboo at 16 with the great master Sakaguchi Sounsai. In 1958 he had a traditional apprenticeship with Tanabe Chikuunsai II; that same year, his work was admitted to the

Japan Modern Arts and Crafts Exhibition where he won the Yomiuri Television Broadcast Award. His work has been accepted numerous times in Nitten and Shin Kogei exhibitions.

Since then he has had numerous solo shows, most recently at the Sasayama Museum of History and Arts, and won the Superior Award at the Kyoto Craft Arts Exhibition. Minoura's baskets are represented in the permanent collection of the Denver Art Museum and Asian Art Museum of San Francisco.

Monden Kogyoku (b. 1916)   p.16–17
Kogyoku, which means "bamboo grove treasure," is Monden's artistic name, given to him when he was 21, a few short years after he began making bamboo baskets. His long and prestigious career has been marked with numerous honors and has been uninterrupted except for two decades after the war when economic turmoil required he make thousands of utilitarian baskets for sale to wholesalers. This period ended when a local department store manager, learning of his reputation, invited him to present an exhibition of flower baskets.

Monden, who lives in Beppu, became a full member of the Japan Traditional Craft Arts Exhibition in 1991, is an active leader in his prefecture, a judge for many regional exhibitions, and a teacher at the community college in Fukuyama City. His work is included in collections at the Denver Art Museum, Asian Art Museum of San Francisco, and Mint Museum of Craft and Design in Charlotte, North Carolina.

The artist tells his students, "Don't imitate others, create your own personal style. And don't be afraid of making mistakes. Even if it's bad, you will gain something in your efforts."

Monden Yuichi (b. 1942)   p.56–57
Monden Yuichi's father, Monden Kogyoku, discouraged him from pursuing a career as a bamboo artist because of the economic hardships of the life. Heeding his advice, Monden Yuichi chose to become an engineer but not before spending countless hours observing his father at work. Although not formally trained, this study gave him the tools he needed to produce one basket a year, which he submitted to local exhibitions.

The bamboo arts were never far from his thoughts. In 1998, when he retired from engineering, he attended the Beppu Occupational School and studied under Tanabe Nobuyuki, a top student of Japanese Living Treasure Shono Shounsei. Then he returned to the Fukuyama area where he was born and dedicated himself to bamboo sculpture.

In 2004, he won the Newcomers Prize at Japan's Gendai Kogei Exhibition and the next year he had his first successful admission in the

prestigious Nitten show. His work is part of the collection at the Museum of Arts and Design in New York City and was represented in *The Next Generation* exhibit at the University of Arkansas.

A marathon runner with an exuberant personality, Monden brings a fresh, vibrant energy to his still-developing work.

Morigami Jin (b. 1955)   p.76–77
One of the most artistically gifted of the younger generation of Japanese bamboo artists, Morigami's parents are both bamboo artisans who work commercially. When he enrolled at the Beppu Occupational School he had a solid foundation in bamboo.

His graduation was fortuitously timed. The Japanese economy was strong and his gentle, delicate designs had broad appeal for decorating modern apartments. For a time, he had so many department store orders that he employed several young assistants. A fine designer and craftsman, Morigami is credited with introducing a new style of bamboo basketry to the Beppu market.

As a young artist he submitted his work to Nitten and, in a highly unusual process, was accepted without having to advance through the interim stages. The resentment that ensued from more senior artists contributed to his decision to end his involvement with Japan's public exhibition system.

By the time his work was introduced to collectors in the United States, he was so consumed with earning a living for his family that he had given up creating new pieces. Today, Western interest has breathed new life into his career. Morigami is working on a series of topography-themed sculpture made in a style of hexagonal plaiting that is a radical departure from the traditional.

His pieces are part of collections at the Denver Art Museum and the Museum of Arts and Design in New York City. In 2004, he was a finalist for the prestigious Cotsen Prize.

Nagakura Kenichi (b. 1952)   p.74–75
"For me it is very important to use parts of a bamboo plant from above ground and parts from below ground," Nagakura says. "I like to add bamboo roots to some of my work as a reminder of the dark side of life."

Unaffiliated with any of Japan's craft arts organizations, Nagakura is the first recipient of the Cotsen Bamboo Prize, awarded in 2000, and an esteemed independent artist for more than 20 years.

His organic, contemporary pieces are rooted in the functional baskets made for centuries for flower arranging at Japanese tea ceremonies but also borrow from wide-ranging sources, including European sculpture, the American pop art movement, indigenous Japanese forms, and cord-patterned clay work from the 3rd and 2nd millennia B.C. His fine plaiting mimics complex line drawing and the graceful shapes of his vessels are inspired by human form and by objects from the natural world, such as fallen leaves, emerging shoots, and cocoons.

Nakagura began his career dyeing fabric for kimonos but quickly realized he wanted to make artwork, like ceramics, that had an inherent vitality. He spent three years splitting bamboo for his grandfather, who was a bamboo wholesaler. Several years later he brought his work to a contemporary gallery that gave him a solo show. He is passionate about jazz, classical, and rock music, and strives to elicit the "rhythm and harmony" of bamboo.

Nakatomi Hajime (b. 1974)   p.88–89

Nakatomi attended one of Japan's top private colleges, the American equivalent of Harvard or Yale. He was a member of the university ceramics club and was a serious student of clay until several events conspired to change the course of his career. He saw a bamboo basket made by Tanabe Chikuunsai II, met the bamboo artist and industrial designer Ohashi in Tokyo, and came upon a book about bamboo fences. The beauty and versatility of bamboo left him awe-struck and, much to his parents' dismay, he decided to attend the Beppu Occupational School to learn bamboo. He later apprenticed to Honda Syoryu.

The youngest artist in this exhibition, Nakatomi's interest is in quiet, delicate vessels that straddle the line between traditional and contemporary styles. A student of sensha tea ceremony, his work has twice garnered the Oita Governor's Prize and, in 2004, the Beppu Mayor's Prize at the 40th Beppu City Bamboo New Works Exhibition. Nakatomi has only recently begun to exhibit at the national level in Japan.

Shono Tokuzo (b. 1942)   p.54–55

A sculpture graduate from Musashino Art University, Shono Tokuzo apprenticed to his father, Shono Shounsai, the first Living National Treasure in bamboo arts.

After his father's death, he was commissioned by the office of the prime minister to make a special white bamboo flower vase to be displayed at the official guest house in Tokyo.

Shono won the grand prize at the Japan New Craft Arts Exhibition in 1984 and 1998, which led to his full membership in the organization. In 1999, he received a grand prize at Nitten, thus taking an important step towards full Nitten membership.

His work is part of collections at the Asian Art Museum of San Francisco, the Oita Prefecture and Oita City museums. One of his pieces is included in Japan's Imperial Household collection.

"As I compose the work I carry an image of transparency, like a work of clear glass," he says. "The purity of the bamboo is what I am looking for, to express the beauty of openness in the work. I want to create something that is original and filled with energy."

Sugita Jozan (b. 1932)   p.32–33

Sugita has overcome numerous challenges to rise to the top of Japan's bamboo art world. At 13, he lost his hearing in an era when disabled people were not well integrated in Japan's public schools. Despite his handicap he pursued an education, eventually studying at a newly established institution for the deaf. He graduated, became a teacher at the school, and earned an art degree through a correspondence course. Sugita is fluent in Japanese, English, and sign language.

An early memory of a farmer making a bamboo basket stayed with him into adulthood. He admired the delicate, hexagonal style of bamboo master Tanabe Chikuunsai II and copied Tanabe's work to learn technique. Gradually, he improved the structural soundness of his baskets and developed a restrained, subtle aesthetic that rewards viewers who are willing to spend time with his pieces.

In addition to achieving full membership in the Traditional Craft Arts Association, Sugita has won numerous major prizes and his work is in permanent collections at the National Museum of Modern Art in Tokyo, Museum of Modern Art in Shiga, and Asian Art Museum of San Francisco. He was also selected as an Intangible Cultural Asset, the local equivalent of Living National Treasure designation.

Tanabe Shochiku III (b. 1973)   p.84–85

Tanabe was born to one of Japan's most prestigious bamboo pedigrees. Like his father, Tanabe Chikuunsai III, he attended art school and earned a degree in sculpture. He is the chosen son, slated to become Tanabe Chikuunsai IV, representing the fourth generation of bamboo artists in his family.

From a young age he gravitated towards bamboo, making his first piece when he was only 7 or 8. He continues to work alongside his esteemed father in the elder's Osaka studio, taking brief breaks in Beppu to improve his proficiency.

His signature is organic sculptural forms made with tiger bamboo and other natural materials. Although only 32, he has received many accolades, including the Mayor's Award at the Sakai City Art Exhibition in 2001 and the Osaka Craft Exhibition Choice Award at the All Kansai Art Exhibition in 2004. He is also active outside Japan, exhibiting and demonstrating in Australia, New Zealand, Switzerland, and Korea. His work is housed at the Seattle Art Museum and Philadelphia Museum

of Art. Recently Lloyd Cotsen, the former CEO of the Neutrogena corporation and a visionary collector of Japanese bamboo, donated one of Tanabe's baskets to the Long Beach Museum of Art.

Tanaka Kyokusho (b. 1947)   p.60–61

Freshly graduated from the Beppu Occupational School, Tanaka built his pieces from the bottom up, in the traditional way. Quickly, however, his work evolved into sleek, minimal objects of great refinement, constructed of thinly sliced, stacked, and threaded rattan and bamboo, a crisscross technique of his own invention.

An admirer of architecture, he constructs his baskets like buildings. Each is fabricated from 30 or more individual parts, occasionally incorporating smoked bamboo from the rafters of 200 year-old houses. Two decades ago, he created an open, airy method of transparent weaving, or *sukashi-ami*, that allows his baskets, as he puts it, to "breathe."

His innovation has been recognized by Japan's Traditional Craft Arts Association, which has admitted him into its annual juried shows nearly every year for more than a quarter-century and awarded him top prizes, including a Chairman's Award, some half-dozen times. One of his pieces was purchased by the Japanese government as a gift for visiting dignitaries.

"The distance between strings is the most important point," the artist says of his construction process. "Even slight differences in distance make a big difference. There are so many combinations. I decide which ones are the most beautiful through the process of trial and error."

Tanioka Aiko (b. 1947)   p.62–63

Tanioka Aiko is one of only a handful of Japanese women to earn recognition in the bamboo arts. Still young to have achieved mastery of her field, Tanioka's designs and technical abilities continue to develop.

She met Tanabe Chikuunsai III in 1985 at an exhibition of his work at a local department store. She stopped to speak to the esteemed bamboo artist about her interest in his baskets and he invited her to his studio. For 15 years, she studied under his tutelage, learning the Tanabe family traditions. Through Tanabe she met another bamboo student, Tanioka Shigeo, who she later married.

Tanioka has exhibited since 2000 in *The Next Generation* at the University of Arkansas and other shows. She has won several awards in Japan, including the Hiramatsu Prize at the Osaka Craft Exhibition and the Nara Education Committee Prize at the Japan Craft Arts Kinki Exhibition.

Tanioka Shigeo (b. 1949) p.68-69

After graduating from design school, Tanioka worked at an advertising company for two years. He was not happy there and one day, in a book, he found a photograph of one of Shono Shounsai's most famous baskets. He decided then and there to study bamboo art. At the age of 25, he apprenticed himself to Tanabe Chikuunsai II and, by 1984, he had become an independent bamboo artist.

Tanioka has won many prestigious awards, including the President's Prize from the Japan Craft Arts Association in 2001. The next year he was a finalist for the Cotsen Bamboo Prize and in 2004 was its sole recipient. His work is part of collections at the Sakai City Museum, Craft Arts Hall in Shiga, Asian Art Museum of San Francisco, and Ruth and Sherman Lee Institute for Japanese Art. He was included in *The Next Generation* at the University of Arkansas.

"The goal of bamboo artists is to show how well you can reconstruct the natural beauty of bamboo through your creativity, originality, and techniques of weaving and plaiting," he says. "To make a piece for exhibition takes months of work. Probably the best analogy I can use to describe this process is climbing a mountain. It is a long and hard process. When you are finally on top, you feel the moment of satisfaction. Yet this satisfaction won't last long."

Torii Ippo (b. 1930) p.30-31

Torii Ippo began his career in bamboo arts at the age of 21, after his father's death. There was no choice for him, since the family business was the only means of support for his family. He taught himself by making copies of his father's baskets.

In 1959, he visited an exhibition of treasures housed at Todaiji Temple in Nara. At the time he was feeling unsure whether he had the talent for bamboo. "I remember how that day my eyes stopped at a bamboo basket that was said to have been used as a flower basket for the memorial service of Emperor Seimu in 757 A.D.," he recalls. "The basket was rather flat-shaped and it had remained in perfect condition for over 1,200 years. Its power instantly charmed me. That moment determined my career as a bamboo artist."

Torii is often selected as a judge for public exhibitions in Japan and has demonstrated bamboo art in Germany. His pieces are in collections at the Nishio City Museum, Nishio Cultural Center, and Mint Museum of Craft and Design in Charlotte, North Carolina. One of his baskets is a promised gift to the Museum of Arts and Design in New York City.

Ueno Masao (b. 1949) p.64-65

Uneo Masao graduated from the Shibaura Institute of Technology with a degree in architecture and studied bamboo with Honma Kazuaki. Since the 1980s, he has exhibited worldwide, installing outdoor pieces at the Grizedale Sculpture Park in England and the University of Zurich's museum park. In 1991, his work was included in *The 20th Contemporary Art Exhibition of Japan* at the Tokyo Metropolitan Art Museum and Kyoto City Museum of Art. His work is part of the Ruth and Sherman Lee Institute for Japanese Art collection.

The artist picks *madake* bamboo in the mountains of Japan, dyes and lacquers the material, and finishes with gold leaf and gold powder, a technique he adapted from traditional wood artists. Tinged in gold, his pieces transform with shifts in light. Many of his ideas are formulated using computer-assisted design software.

Watanabe Shochikusai II (b. 1927) p.22-23

When his parents died of tuberculosis, Watanabe went to live with an uncle who often visited Beppu and brought back bamboo flower baskets. In 1941, Watanabe graduated from high school and was sent to Beppu to learn bamboo crafts under Kadota Niko. There, he met Watanabe Shochikusai I, who was famous for his twill plaited boxes, and became his apprentice. After the war, Watanabe worked with Watanabe I, was adopted into the family, and succeeded the artist's name.

In 1980, the Ministry of Economy, Trade and Industry recognized him as a Traditional Craft Arts Skill Holder, and the next year, the Imperial family purchased his work. His pieces, which continue the signature twill plaiting of his mentor, are part of collections at the Beppu Art Museum, Oita Prefecture Art Hall, and Beppu City Traditional Bamboo Center.

"Quite honestly, I consider myself an artisan," he says. "I only work in twill plaiting, but within this limitation I always push myself to a new innovation. Beauty to me is not static, it is dynamic. Thinking of patterns, color coordination, and proportions all the time keeps my mind young and flexible. I am happy when I succeed in a new innovation, but I am happier if people like the work and value it."

Yako Hodo (b. 1940) p.44-45

Yako learned the basics of bamboo technique at vocational school and continued his studies as an apprentice to masters Nakajima Hoso, Nakamura Yukosai, and Baba Shodo. Within a decade, while he was still in his 20s, his work garnered major awards, culminating in 2000 with a prestigious medal given by the Emperor and the Japanese government.

Yako, who lives in Saitama prefecture in the Tokyo region, has exhibited at the Asian Art Museum of San Francisco, Honolulu Academy of Art, and in *Best Bamboo Baskets: the Cotsen Collection* at LongHouse Reserve in East Hampton, New York.

"When I make a basket, I draw rough sketches first to conceptualize the image I would like to capture," Yako says. "When I have a hard time finding out what adjustments to make, I try listening to the bamboo and asking it what I should do. It is important to improve one's skills and techniques but mental preparation and conceptualization are just as important. The baskets I make reflect both function and dream."

Yamaguchi Ryuun (b. 1940) p.46-47

Yamaguchi graduated in bamboo craft from the Beppu Occupational School in 1957 and, at 23, apprenticed to Living National Treasure Shono Shounsai.

A decade later he began receiving accolades, garnering the Beppu City Mayor's Award and Oita Prefecture Governor's Awards. Between 1966 and 2004, he won more than 25 important prizes. His work has been purchased by the Oita Prefectural Art Hall, Oita City Museum of Art, and Mint Museum of Craft and Design and exhibited in *Best Bamboo Baskets: the Cotsen Collection* at LongHouse Reserve in East Hampton, New York.

"Frankly speaking, I never thought of the possibility of being an artist until I apprenticed with the first Living National Treasure in bamboo arts, Shono Shounsai," he says. "His example deeply inspired me to express myself. Even now, it is a great struggle for me with each new piece. I feel the beauty of the flowers. I feel the beauty of the water flow. I try to bring that flow into my pattern. At first I was very surprised that people wanted to collect my work in the West, but now it has given me more confidence as an artist."

Yufu Shohaku (b. 1941) p.50-51

Yufu is a second generation bamboo artist from Beppu, the son of Yufu Tadashi. His father apprenticed to Sato Chikuyusai, who was the teacher of bamboo master Shono Shounsai.

The artist began making baskets in elementary school and achieved mastery by middle school. With his father, he created many styles of flower baskets that made Beppu famous. Today he is known for traditional Beppu rough-plaited baskets that blend plant roots and bamboo chunks.

Yufu taught his popular basket techniques to many students and generously allowed them to sell copies of his work, even when the copies became more popular with wholesalers. Many of his friends told him not to let others take advantage but his response was "My father told me to help others and that's what I am doing."

An independent artist, he is the leader of his local bamboo art association and the recipient of numerous prizes, include the Beppu Mayor's Special Recognition Award and Chairman's Prize at the Traditional Craft Arts Exhibition.

His work is in the collection of the Beppu City Traditional Bamboo Center.

BIBLIOGRAPHY

Austin, Robert and Koichiro Ueda. *Bamboo*.
New York and Tokyo: Weatherhill, 1970.

Bess, Nancy Moore. *Bamboo in Japan*.
Tokyo: Kodansha International, 2001.

Brauen, Martin. *Bamboo in Old Japan,
Art and Culture on the Threshold to Modernity,
The Hans Sporry Collection in the Ethnographic
Museum of Zurich Univerity*. Stuttgart: Arnoldsche
Art Publishers, 2003.

Coffland, Robert T. *Contemporary Japanese Bamboo
Arts*. Chicago and Santa Fe: Art Media Resources
and TAI Gallery, 1999.

Coffland, Robert T. "Japanese Bamboo Arts."
Arts of Asia, Volume 29, Number 2, 1999.

Coffland, Robert T. "Energy and Strength in
Balance: The Bamboo Basket Art of Fujinuma
Noboru." *Orientations*, Volume 30, Number 2,
February 1999.

Cort, Louise Allison and Kenji Nakamura.
A Basketmaker in Rural Japan. Washington D.C.
and New York: Smithsonian Institution and
Weatherhill, 1994.

Cotsen, Lloyd and Robert Coffland. *The Bamboo
Basket Art of Higashi Takesonosai*. Los Angeles:
Cotsen Occasional Press, 2002.

Cotsen, Lloyd, Janet Koplos, Patricia J. Graham,
Hiroko Johnson, and Moroyama Masanori.
*Japanese Bamboo Baskets: Masterworks of Form
and Texture*. Edited by Joseph N. Newland.
Los Angeles: Cotsen Occasional Press, 1999.

Farrelly, David. *The Book of Bamboo*.
San Francisco: Sierra Club Books, 1984.

Kahlenberg, Mary Hunt, and Mark Schwartz.
A Book About Grass: Its Beauty and Uses.
New York: E.P. Dutton, 1983.

Kaneko Kenji and Moroyama Masanori. *Take no
kogei: kindai ni okeru tenkai* (Modern bamboo craft:
Developments in the modern era). Tokyo: Tokyo
National Museum of Modern Art, 1985.

McCallum, Toshiko M. *Containing Beauty:
Japanese Bamboo Flower Baskets*. Los Angeles:
UCLA Museum of Cultural History, 1988.

AUTHORS' BIOGRAPHIES

Robert T. Coffland first visited
Japan in 1982. Within the last ten years,
he changed careers from the food industry
to writing, researching, and selling Japanese
bamboo arts. He and his wife, Mary Hunt
Kahlenberg, an expert in textiles, own TAI
Gallery in Santa Fe. From his home in Santa
Fe, Coffland travels extensively to promote
the art and artists found in this catalogue.
He develops public and private collections
of Japanese bamboo arts, and curates
exhibitions to bring this work to a wider
audience.

Donald B. Doe has a Ph.D. from
Ohio University in Comparative Arts.
His interdisciplinary degree has been an
excellent foundation for a career in
Midwestern art museums, where he has
overseen collections ranging from Roman
antiquities to contemporary regional art.
As a curator and museum director, he has
organized numerous exhibitions and written
widely on art. This is his first venture into
Asian art. Doe is a lecturer at Grinnell
College and a free-lance curator living in
Grinnell, Iowa.

Daniel Strong is the associate director
and curator of exhibitions for the Faulconer
Gallery, Grinnell College. As one of his
many tasks on a small staff, he serves as
the in-house photographer, putting an
undergraduate art degree to good use.
He curates exhibitions of contemporary
sculpture, photography, painting, and
drawing. He previously worked at
museums in Rochester, New York,
Amherst, Massachusetts and Northampton,
Massachusetts (Smith College). He has
lived and worked in Grinnell since 1999.